Best Eas

# Best Easy Day Hikes
# Northern Virginia

## Louise S. Baxter

**FALCON**GUIDES

GUILFORD, CONNECTICUT

# FALCONGUIDES®

An imprint of The Rowman & Littlefield Publishing Group, Inc.
4501 Forbes Blvd., Ste. 200
Lanham, MD 20706
www.rowman.com
Falcon and FalconGuides are registered trademarks and Make Adventure Your Story is a trademark of The Rowman & Littlefield Publishing Group, Inc.

Distributed by NATIONAL BOOK NETWORK

Maps by Melissa Baker

British Library Cataloguing-in-Publication Information Available

Library of Congress Control Number: 2020950439

ISBN 978-1-4930-5117-5 (paper)
ISBN 978-1-4930-5118-2 (electronic)

# Contents

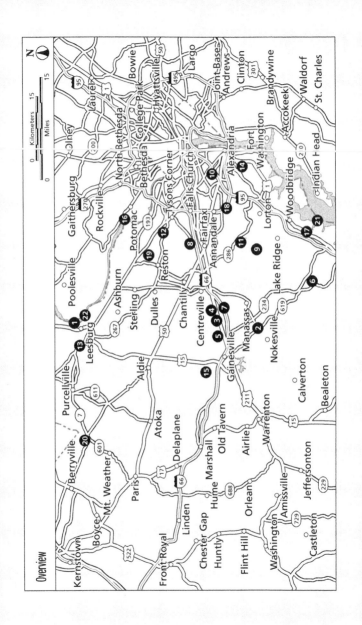

Overview

# Acknowledgments

I want to express my great appreciation for the National Park Service, Virginia State Parks, county park authorities, and private preservation organizations that do a fantastic job teaching us about history and nature, and work hard to preserve these parks. It is because of their efforts that we, and future generations, can continue to enjoy all that this region has to offer. Many thanks to my friends for their support and their great ideas for hikes. And a special thanks to my late father, Craig Baxter, who bestowed in me a love for history and words.

# Introduction

For 12,000 years, people have been exploring the region that is now called Northern Virginia. Many Native American tribes lived here, with its streams and forests abundant with food and rivers to navigate for trade. Captain John Smith set out to map the region in 1608, and since then it has grown steadily into farmland, cities, and now a giant metropolis outside the nation's capital. It is remarkable that in such a tightly developed area, there are still spaces to breathe fresh air, listen to birds and frogs, and see fields of wildflowers.

Northern Virginia, by most definitions, encompasses the counties of Arlington, Fairfax, Loudoun, and Prince William; and the cities of Alexandria, Fairfax, Falls Church, and Manassas. In 1736, this land was part of a deed given to Lord Fairfax, a name seen all over this region. Lord Fairfax lived with his brother in Belvoir, now Fort Belvoir, until he built a lodge, named Greenway, near what is now the city of Winchester. It was here he met a young man named George Washington and hired him to begin surveying the western part of his land. When the Declaration of Independence was signed, Lord Fairfax was in his 80s, and he remained neutral during the Revolutionary War. He died shortly after the Battle of Yorktown and the end of the war.

The Washington-Rochambeau Revolutionary Route crosses the area. This was a 680-mile series of trails taken by the Continental Army from New England to Yorktown, Virginia, where the British were defeated in 1781. The route travels over the Occoquan River and through what is now Prince William Park.

After independence, the design for a federal city was drawn up that originally included parts of Maryland and

Virginia. Boundary stones dating back to this time can still be seen in Arlington and Alexandria. A problem arose when citizens on the Virginia side were unhappy with the idea of lack of representation if they were part of a federal city and that the federal city abolished slavery. The Virginia portion of the land that became Washington, D.C., was never incorporated as part of the capital city and was given back by Congress in 1846.

Tensions continued throughout the nineteenth century between Northern and Southern states culminating in the American Civil War, which broke out in April 1861. Virginia seceded and joined the Confederate States, but Maryland, also a slave-holding state, remained with the Union. The proximity of the two capitals—Washington, D.C., and Richmond—led to this region being the site of several critical battles. Skirmishes along the Potomac River and several battles around Manassas represent some of the Civil War history of Northern Virginia featured in several hikes in this book. Today they provide a history lesson along with a chance to hike and reflect on all that was sacrificed.

As the nation moved into the twentieth century, Northern Virginia grew as companies were established to support the federal government, technology advanced, and suburbs bloomed as people wanted to have more room to raise their families. New housing areas led to new commercial areas, such as the planned town of Reston, Tysons Corners, and the Dulles Corridor. The area is a sprawling mixture of residential, industrial, and commercial communities, but, fortunately, a lot of effort has been made to preserve historic and natural areas.

You can't walk very far anywhere in Northern Virginia without coming across a historic spot. Historical markers are found everywhere, from trails to inner city streets to suburban parking lots. The natural beauty of the region is highlighted in the mountains, streams, and wetlands, and has created fascinating places to learn and to appreciate the local flora and fauna. More than half of the hikes in this book focus on natural preservation and education. Many streams in the area are referred to as "runs." There is a lot of debate about the word, but basically, it's just a local reference for stream or creek.

A booming industry in Northern Virginia is the wine and beer business. Many of the hikes are near local wineries and breweries, perfect places to chill out after some time on the trail. Wineries can be searched at www.virginiawine .org and breweries at www.virginia.org/beertrails. In addition, some hikes are close to charming towns like Leesburg, Manassas, Occoquan, and Alexandria. All are delightful places to grab a bite to eat or shop. Others are near famous landmarks, such as historic houses. Each hike description includes nearby places to visit.

There is a lot to see and do in Northern Virginia, so make a plan and head outside!

## Weather

Northern Virginia is in the mid-Atlantic region, which has a humid climate. The area is known for its hot and sticky summers and milder winters with a few snowfalls without a lot of accumulation. Every hike in this book can certainly be done any time of the year. Spring and fall usually have comfortable temperatures and are the ideal seasons for hiking. In summer try to walk in the morning or evening. Winter days can be clear and crisp in this region, so a hike is a great idea to get some fresh air. Choose trails that have more open spaces to take advantage of the winter sun; while the area is not known for a lot of snow, some of these trails are great for snowshoeing, particularly on fresh snow.

It's best to dress in layers regardless of the season. In winter, even if it's freezing out, you will warm up once you get moving. In summer, lighter clothes perhaps with long sleeves and pants work best when out where ticks and other bugs are around. In spring and fall, the temps in the early morning can be chilly but warm up considerably after the sun is overhead.

Trails, especially those that include a waterway, can get buggy, so bring some repellent. The sun can be strong, too, even in winter; consequently, wear sunscreen and a hat, especially on trails that are out in the open.

## Traffic

Traffic in this region is manageable with some planning. Morning rush hour runs from 6 to 9 a.m. and evening from 3 to 7 p.m. However, many of these hikes are far enough away from the city to be too badly affected. Using your GPS, check the best route and maybe plan a little extra time to get around. The directions given with each hike, in particular the major roads used, are guidelines, as there are usually several ways to reach a destination.

Also, some roads have strict rush-hour restrictions on weekdays, except major holidays, particularly I-66, where there is a high-occupancy vehicle (HOV) lane; only cars with two or more people are permitted to use this lane. On I-495, the Capital Beltway, there are express lanes that require an E-ZPass and charge different rates, which are posted, depending on time of day and traffic.

Every hike in this book has nearby parking, almost always for free. Public transportation isn't readily available to these areas.

## Zero Impact

Most of the trails in this book are maintained by governmental or private organizations and are well-conserved. Please take care when you visit to preserve the areas for others.

- Stay on the designated trails. Many off-trail areas are not safe, or they may be in the location of regeneration projects.

- Don't leave anything behind; pack your trash and discard it in a trash receptacle, if available, or take it with you when you leave the park.

- Be careful of wild animals and don't feed them.

- Leave flowers, rocks, and other "souvenirs" behind. Take only pictures and memories.

- Be mindful of other users of the trails. Some trails are also used by cyclists, runners, and horseback riders.

- Keep your noise level at a minimum. Shouting can be startling to wildlife and other humans.

- Dogs are permitted on many of the trails. They must be on leashes no longer than 6 feet, and please pick up after them.

- Please do not smoke on the trails. It's not expressly prohibited, but it can mar the enjoyment of other trail users.

## Safety

The trails featured here are short and often near populated areas where help is readily available. However, should anything happen, cell service is accessible from most of the trails. Carry a phone with you in case of any emergency, but keep it on vibrate or a low ring so others aren't disturbed.

Always carry, and drink, water. It's easy to get dehydrated quickly throughout any season, but especially so on the hot days of the summer. Carry a basic first-aid kit that includes antiseptic and bandages for scrapes.

Watch out for poison ivy. It grows well in this area and is often seen along the trails. The plant has three pointy leaves; the largest is in the middle. The leaves are usually a bit shiny and range in color from red in the spring to green in summer and yellow in fall. If you stay on the trails, you should be able to avoid it.

Any information about hiking in the mid-Atlantic needs to address the prevalence of ticks. The chances of encountering ticks in this region are highest during spring and summer and in open fields, but it's always a good idea to check yourself after hiking anywhere, any time of the year. If you're on a hike through an open field, try to walk in the center of the trail to stay away from the longer grasses. Use insect repellent with DEET and wear long pants and shirtsleeves if it's not too hot. Check for ticks as soon as you return home. Also check your canine pals! Ticks can be carefully removed with tweezers; pull it up straight to make sure it's all out. If you find a tick and are concerned about what kind it is, the Fairfax County Health Department will identify them. More information can be found at www.fairfaxcounty.gov/health/fightthebite/tick-identification.

If you are going to hike alone, please let someone know where you are going and when. Some hikes in this book start at visitor centers, and you can always advise someone there about where you're going. It's also a good idea to text a friend and let them know where you are and when you expect to return. And then be sure to text them when you return so they know you're all right.

# How to Use This Guide

This guide is designed to give concise information about the area of each hike and to answer common questions about each trail. Each hike will give the total distance, a detailed breakdown of distances and directions, and a map. Admission fees and times, type of trail, other uses of the trail, and additional helpful information is listed with each hike. Park websites are also provided; it's a good idea to check these ahead of time in case there are any special events or closures when you are planning to visit.

The hikes in this guide were chosen for their accessibility, easy ability level, and scenic and historic value. Some are in wooded, natural areas, while others are out in open fields or in nature preserves. Some pass by historic places, and others have amazing views.

## Selecting a Hike

The hikes in this book are all considered easy hikes, but *easy* is a relative term. A few hikes are listed as "easy to moderate," which only means they might have a bit more elevation or go over rougher terrain. Most hikes are in the 1- to 3-mile range; however, there are a few that are longer, but they are generally easy to walk. A good pair of sneakers is enough to navigate the trails.

The book covers a wide variety of trails, including quiet walks in the woods, historic sites, wildlife preserves, and gardens. All hikes are within a 1.5-hour drive of Washington, D.C., and most are closer. With each hike description are ideas of what other attractions are in the area if you want to spend a little extra time.

Keep in mind that what you think is easy is entirely dependent on your level of fitness and the adequacy of your gear (primarily shoes). Use the trail's length as a gauge of its relative difficulty—even if climbing is involved, it won't be bad if the hike is less than 1 mile. If you are hiking with a group, select a hike that is appropriate for everyone.

## Hiker Checklist

Because these hikes are short and easy, you won't need to carry a lot of gear. In general, you should have the following with you:

- Full water bottle
- Cell phone
- First-aid kit
- Hat

Before you leave your car, apply sunscreen and insect repellant. You might want to consider some kind of snack, too, but check the hike details first to make sure that food is allowed. Lastly, be sure your cell phone is fully charged so that you can take a lot of photos!

# Trail Finder

### Best Hikes for History
1. Ball's Bluff Battlefield
2. Bristoe Station
3. Henry Hill
4. Stone Bridge
5. Brawner Farm
21. Leesylvania State Park
22. Red Rock Wilderness

### Best Hikes for Nature Lovers
6. Prince William Forest
7. Bull Run Bluebell Trail
9. Fountainhead Trail
13. Rust Nature Sanctuary
14. Huntley Meadows Park
16. Riverbend Park

### Best Hikes for Scenic Views
10. Winkler Botanical Preserve
12. Meadowlark Gardens
17. Neabsco Creek
20. Bears Den Overlook

### Best Hikes for Relaxation
8. Difficult Run Stream Valley Trail
11. Burke Lake
15. Silver Lake
18. Lake Accotink
19. Lake Anne

# Map Legend

## Municipal

- ═╡95╞═ Interstate Highway
- ═╡17╞═ US Highway
- ═╡28╞═ State Highway
- ═╡677╞═ Local Road
- ═ ═ ═ ═ Unpaved Road
- ├──+──+──┤ Railroad
- ─ ─ · ─ · State Line
- ────── Leader Line

## Trails

- ▒▒▒▒▒▒ Featured Road
- ▬ ▬ ▬ ▬ Featured Trail
- ─ ─ ─ ─ Trail
- ▐▐▐▐▐▐▐▐ Boardwalk/Steps

## Water Features

-  Body of Water
- ∿ River/Creek
- ≋ Waterfall

## Land Management

- 🔺 National Battlefield Park
- 🔺 State/Regional Park/Forest/Preserve

## Symbols

- 🛥 Boat Ramp
- ⏝ Bridge
- ▲ Campground
- ▮ Gate
- → Hike Arrows
- ▱ Inn/Lodging
- ▲ Mountain/Peak
- 🅿 Parking
- 🌳 Picnic Area
- ■ Point of Interest/Structure
- 🚻 Restrooms
- 🍴 Restaurant
- ♜ Tower
- ○ Town
- ⓫ Trailhead
- 📷 Viewpoint/Overlook
- ❷ Visitor/Information Center
- 🐎 Stables

# 1   Ball's Bluff Battlefield

The Battle of Ball's Bluff happened by accident, not plan, and resulted in the death of a US senator and 223 Union soldiers.

**Main interest:** History

**Distance:** 2.3-mile loop

**Hiking time:** About 2 hours

**Difficulty:** Easy

**Trail surface:** Natural surfaces

**Best season:** Year-round; great for fall foliage

**Other trail users:** None

**Canine compatibility:** Dogs allowed on leash

**Fees and permits:** None

**Schedule:** Daily dawn to dusk

**Facilities:** None

**Map:** www.novaparks.com/sites/default/files/maps/trailmapballsbluff.pdf

**Trail contact:** Ball's Bluff Battlefield Regional Park, Ball's Bluff Road, Leesburg 20176; (703) 737-7800; www.novaparks.com/parks/balls-bluff-battlefield-regional-park

**Finding the Trailhead:** From VA 7 west, turn right on Battlefield Parkway NE. Follow for about 3 miles to Ball's Bluff Road NE. Turn right and continue on this road until you reach the park entrance; go straight to the parking lot. GPS: N39 07.819' / W77 31.860'

## The Hike

In October 1861, Union and Confederate troops were camped on opposite sides of the Potomac River. The Confederate camp was here at Ball's Bluff. When Union general Stone received a message to make a "slight demonstration" to convince the South to retreat, he sent a scout party ahead to determine the exact location of the rebel camp. In the dark, they mistakenly identified a group of trees as the enemy camp; meanwhile, the Confederates were able to observe them and prepare for the attack. The next morning, October 21, 1861, the prepared Confederates successfully forced Union troops back down the 80-foot bluff. Several Union soldiers died in the river trying to escape. Congress blamed Stone for the defeat, and he was imprisoned, his military career ruined. The fear of similar consequences prevented other Union commanders from taking such decisive action in other battles. Most historians believe that Stone was not to blame, but was a scapegoat to avenge the huge losses in the battle.

Oliver Wendell Holmes was wounded at the Battle of Ball's Bluff but survived and went on to become the oldest serving justice of the US Supreme Court. Colonel Edward Baker, a US senator and lifelong friend of President Abraham Lincoln, died at the battle, the only US senator ever killed in action.

The hike takes you around the perimeter of the battlefield to an overlook of the Potomac River. Because of thick foliage, the river views are best in late fall, winter, and early spring. After the overlook, you will descend a short incline to the river before arriving at the Ball's Bluff National Cemetery, where fifty-three unknown Union soldiers are interred. Only one soldier has been identified, James Allen of the 15th Massachusetts. Near the cemetery are monuments to a Confederate sergeant, Clinton Hatcher, and a Union commander, Senator Edward Baker. Across from the cemetery, a marker shows the spot where Senator Baker was killed. Along the route are several interpretive signs, and guided tours are offered on weekends during the summer months.

Ball's Bluff battlefield is about 10 minutes from downtown Leesburg, a charming eighteenth-century town with shops and restaurants that are perfect for a post-hike stop.

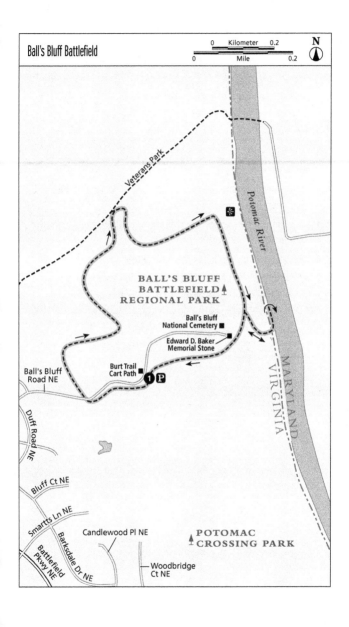

Ball's Bluff Battlefield

| 0 | Kilometer | 0.2 |
| 0 | Mile | 0.2 |

N

Veterans Park

Potomac River

BALL'S BLUFF
BATTLEFIELD
REGIONAL PARK

Ball's Bluff
National Cemetery ■

Edward D. Baker
Memorial Stone

Burt Trail
Cart Path ■

Ball's Bluff
Road NE

1 P

Duff Road NE

Bluff Ct NE

Smartts Ln NE

Candlewood Pl NE

Battlefield Pkwy NE

Barksdale Dr NE

Woodbridge
Ct NE

POTOMAC
CROSSING PARK

MARYLAND

VIRGINIA

Or head up US 15 North for a stop at a winery along the Potomac Cluster of the Loudoun County wine trail; visit the website for more details: www.visitloudoun.org/drink/wine-country/clusters/. Information on the town of Leesburg can be found at www.leesburgva.gov.

## Miles and Directions

**0.0**  Begin at the west end of the parking lot and follow the trail marked with orange.

**1.0**  Make a stop at the top of the bluff for a nice view of the Potomac River. There is a bench there.

**1.1**  Turn left at the sign for the river and walk down the steep slope to the river's edge.

**1.4**  Return back up the hill to the orange trail.

**1.7**  Walk to the open field. The cemetery is on your right and the monument to Senator Baker is on your left.

**1.8**  Continue on the white trail back to the parking lot.

**2.3**  Arrive back at the parking lot.

# 2  Bristoe Station

Two small battles of the Civil War were fought here—the Battle of Kettle Run and the Battle of Bristoe Station—during the time between the two Battles of Bull Run, not far away.

**Main interest:** History

**Distance:** 1.2-mile loop

**Hiking time:** About 1.5 hours

**Difficulty:** Easy

**Trail surface:** Natural surfaces

**Best season:** Year-round; open fields can get hot in the summer.

**Other trail users:** Runners, horses

**Canine compatibility:** Dogs allowed on leash

**Fees and permits:** None

**Schedule:** Daily dawn to dusk

**Facilities:** None

**Map:** www.visitpwc.com/listing/bristoe-station-battlefield-heritage-park/378/

**Trail contact:** Bristoe Station Battlefield Heritage Park, 107089 Bristow Rd., Bristow 20136; (703) 257-5243; www.pwcgov.org/government/dept/park/hp/Pages/Bristoe-Station-Battlefield.aspx

**Finding the Trailhead:** From I-66 West, take VA 234 South (exit 44). Go 4.5 miles and then turn right on VA 28. Go 1.5 miles and turn left on Bristow Road. In 0.25 mile, turn right onto Iron Brigade Unit Avenue, and the parking lot will be on the left at the traffic circle. GPS: N38 43.242' / W77 32.305'

## The Hike

This area of the battlefield park sits adjacent to the tracks of the Alexandria and Orange Railroad, which was established in the 1850s to link Washington, D.C., with southern Virginia. When the Civil War broke out, the rail line was crucial to both sides as it connected both the US capital city and the Confederate capital in Richmond, Virginia, and could carry supplies to troops. Control of the railroad changed hands often, and by the end of the war, it was in shambles. Today the tracks are used for commercial cargo and passenger trains, including the VRE (Virginia Railway Express) commuter trains to Washington.

After the First Battle of Bull Run, Confederate troops set up camp around here, along the railroad tracks. There was an overall lack of sanitation, and many soldiers died of disease. Two small cemeteries have been discovered in the park, although it is believed many more exist due to the high death count. The Battle of Kettle Run was fought on August 27, 1862, and was led by Stonewall Jackson, who had secured the railroad and nearby food warehouses for his troops encamped here. The fight was short and successful for him, and it became the first battle in the Second Manassas series. After the Battle of Gettysburg in July 1863, Confederate troops, commanded by Robert E. Lee, were preparing to make another attack on Bull Run. This never happened because the Battle of Bristoe Station was fought on October 14, 1863, when Confederate troops, led by General A. P. Hill, were camped here. Union forces flanked the camp, approaching from the creek and from the railroad, and overtook them.

The open areas of this battlefield are quite hot in the summer, so early morning is the best time to come. The hike is especially perfect for fall and winter hikes any time of the day, and spring brings beautiful wildflowers to the once war-torn field. Interpretive signs along the way tell the details of the Civil War battles fought here.

Following your historical hike, you might want to visit the town of Manassas. It's a 15-minute drive from Bristoe

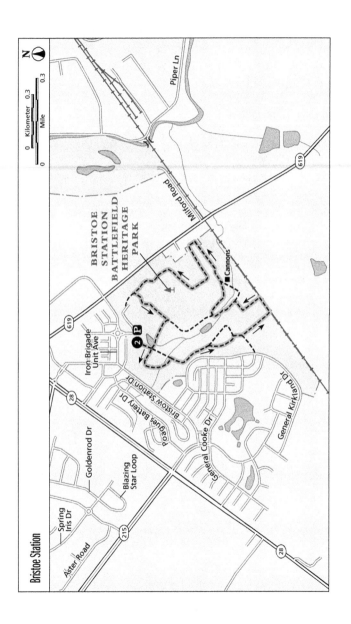

Bristoe Station

Station, and the small town has a lot to offer, including First Friday events, places to eat, and a museum to learn more about the history of the town. Go to http://visitmanassas.org/ for more information.

## Miles and Directions

**0.0** Begin at the parking lot and walk south along a wide trail into the woods.

**0.1** Take a look at a typical soldier's cabin before turning right to follow the trail.

**0.2** Stop at the cemetery sites for the Alabama and Mississippi regiments before continuing, following the trail markers across the battlefield and up to a hill with cannons.

**1.0** From the cannons, walk back to the parking lot.

**1.2** Arrive back at the parking lot.

# 3  Henry Hill

There are two ways of referring to the battle fought in this park—the Union army called it the Battle of Bull Run, and the Confederate army called it the Battle of Manassas. They both are about the same day, and the Union defeat indicated that the war would not be easily won.

**Main interest:** History
**Distance:** 1.2-mile loop
**Hiking time:** About 1.5 hours
**Difficulty:** Easy
**Trail surface:** Natural surfaces
**Best season:** Year-round; some open areas, so go early or late on hot days.
**Other trail users:** None
**Canine compatibility:** Dogs allowed on leash
**Fees and permits:** None

**Schedule:** Daily dawn to dusk; visitor center open daily 8:30 a.m. to 5 p.m., except Thanksgiving Day and Christmas Day.
**Facilities:** Restrooms and drinking water in the visitor center
**Map:** www.nps.gov/mana/plan yourvisit/maps.htm
**Trail contact:** Manassas National Battlefield Park, 12521 Lee Hwy., Manassas 20109; (703) 361-1339; www.nps.gov/mana/index .htm

**Finding the Trailhead:** From I-66 West, take exit 47B onto VA 234 North toward Manassas National Battlefield Park. After 1 mile, turn right at the entrance to the park, then left into the parking lot. GPS: N38 8148' / W77 5219'

## The Hike

The First Battle of Bull Run was fought on this hill in July 1861, only a few months after the start of the war at Fort Sumter, South Carolina, in April. The Union army wanted to make its way south to the Confederate capital at Richmond, Virginia, believing this would bring a quick end to the war. Expecting the Confederate army to be somewhat disorganized, the Union army assumed the battle would be fast and victorious. In fact, families from Washington, D.C., came for the day to have a picnic and watch the battle. Things didn't go as planned, however, and the civilians scrambled back to their carriages to escape, creating chaos and, perhaps, the Washington area's first traffic jam! The Southern newspapers reported this as "the Great Skedaddle."

The walk begins at the visitor center, where there is a small museum, a film, and a bookstore. On the other side of the visitor center, join the trail by walking toward Henry House past several cannons. Henry House, rebuilt after the war, was the home of Judith Carter Henry. Mrs. Henry was 85 years old and stayed in her house during the battle. She was struck by artillery and died hours later, the only civilian killed. Her grave is in a small cemetery next to the house. Also on the grounds is a monument to the Union soldiers who died in the first battle. From the house, look across the field toward VA 29, and you can see the Stone House. An older building was used in the 1820s as a toll stop on a road between Fairfax and Warrenton, where travelers could get a meal and lodging. The house here was built in 1848 as part of the Matthews farm. During the first battle, the Stone House was taken over by the Union army as a hospital, likely because of its sturdy construction and location on the main road. However, later on, the Southerners were able to take over Stone House and it then became a Confederate hospital, and the surviving Union soldiers were taken as prisoners. The house served as a hospital again during the Second Battle of Bull Run, and upstairs, two Union soldiers

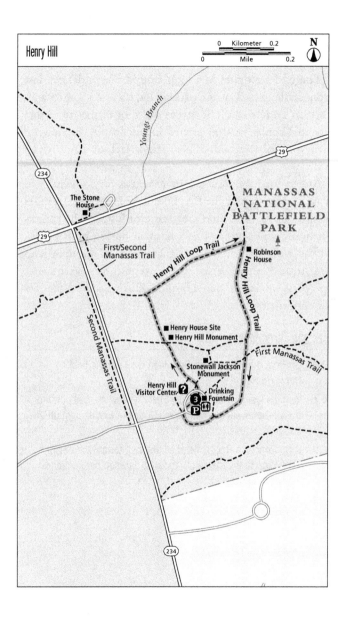

Henry Hill

0     Kilometer    0.2

0         Mile        0.2

**N**

*Youngs Branch*

The Stone House

MANASSAS
NATIONAL
BATTLEFIELD
PARK

Robinson House

First/Second Manassas Trail

Henry Hill Loop Trail

Henry Hill Loop Trail

Second Manassas Trail

Henry House Site
Henry Hill Monument

First Manassas Trail

Stonewall Jackson Monument

Henry Hill Visitor Center

Drinking Fountain

**3**
**P**

carved their names into the floor. Stone House is open for tours; check the National Park Service website or the visitor center for details.

The trail continues in a loop around the battlefield. Just before arriving back at the parking lot, there is a large statue of a man on horseback. It was at this spot in the battle that General Thomas Jackson earned his nickname "Stonewall," when General Bee said, "There stands Jackson like a stone wall."

After your hike, visit nearby Manassas for something to eat, or perhaps stop by the Ben Lomond House, just 2.5 miles down the road, for a little more taste of history. The plantation home was also used as a hospital during both battles, and the walls are covered in signatures from the men who were treated there. Visit www.pwcgov.org/government/ dept/park/hp/Pages/Ben-Lomond-Historic-Site.aspx for more information.

## Miles and Directions

- **0.0** Begin at the visitor center and then walk out the back to Henry House.
- **0.1** Visit the graves and monument here. Follow the trail north to a spot that overlooks Matthews Hill before turning right up to Robinson House.
- **0.5** From Robinson House, head south back toward the beginning. Stop at the statue of Stonewall Jackson before returning to the parking lot.
- **1.2** Arrive back at the parking lot.

# 4 Stone Bridge

Manassas National Battlefield Park today is a significant reminder of the battles fought here and the lives lost. But it's also important to remember that before 1861, this area consisted of family farms, many of which were destroyed in the process of war.

**Main interest:** History, bird watching

**Distance:** 1.4-mile loop

**Hiking time:** About 1.5 hours

**Difficulty:** Easy

**Trail surface:** Natural surfaces, boardwalk

**Best season:** Year-round; nice fall foliage and spring wildflowers

**Other trail users:** Runners

**Canine compatibility:** Dogs allowed on leash

**Fees and permits:** None

**Schedule:** Daily dawn to dusk

**Facilities:** None

**Map:** www.nps.gov/mana/plan yourvisit/maps.htm

**Trail contact:** Manassas National Battlefield Park, 12521 Lee Hwy., Manassas 20109; (703) 361-1339; www.nps.gov/mana/index .htm

**Finding the Trailhead:** From I-66 West, take exit 52 onto US 29 toward Centreville. In 3 miles, just past the entrance sign for the Winery at Bull Run, turn right into the parking lot. Note: If you cross over the creek, you have gone too far. GPS: N38 49.510 / W77 30.127

## The Hike

The first shots at the First Battle of Manassas were fired across the stone bridge over Bull Run. The skirmish here was meant to be a distraction to the Confederates, as Union troops were moving in from farther upstream at Sudley Ford.

The following spring, Confederates destroyed the bridge to prevent Northern troops from using it again. However, the Union troops then constructed a wooden bridge over the original stone foundation. While the bridge was not part of the Second Battle of Bull Run, it came in handy when the Union army had to retreat quickly after their defeat. The bridge that's here today is built in the same style as the original and was completed in 1884.

Before you cross the bridge, walk down to a viewing point with historical information and, in winter and early spring, a nice view of the bridge. In summer and fall, the view is somewhat obstructed by trees on this side. Follow the trail over the bridge and turn right. Walk down any of the small pathways to the creek's edge for better views of the bridge. Continue on the trail next to the water to a short incline to have a look at Farm Ford. This is the spot where Colonel William Sherman led Union troops across the creek, having discovered it was shallow in that section because a reckless Confederate officer had stood there yelling at him and, thereby, demonstrated the ease of crossing.

From here, follow the trail as it heads south through an open meadow to the site of the Van Pelt House. The family who lived here were Union loyalists from New Jersey who had only been there for about ten years. It is rumored that the first shot of the battle landed in their house. They remained on their farm through the Second Battle of Manassas, when Union troops took over the house to use as a hospital. Shortly after that, their son became a Union scout while the elder Van Pelts moved back to New Jersey, leaving their daughter Elizabeth to manage the farm. After the war, she tried, unsuccessfully, to claim damages. The house is gone

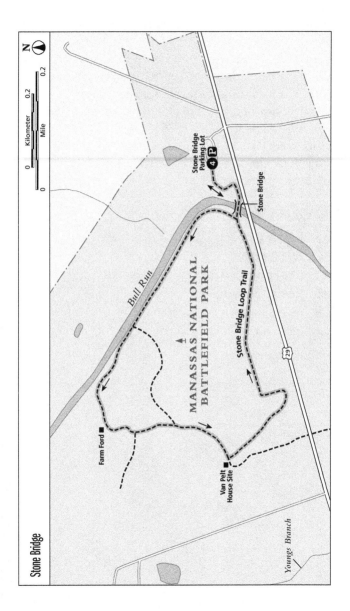

Stone Bridge

now, but the site remains a reminder of the everyday lives that were disrupted when war came to their homes.

Continue on the trail down a steep slope onto a boardwalk over a marsh. In spring you can see bluebells and the flowering redbud trees, and the wetland provides some interesting bird watching. This will bring you back to the bridge. Cross over and return to the parking lot.

Like other hikes in this park, a visit to the town of Manassas is a great way to relax afterward. There is also a winery right next to the parking lot.

## Miles and Directions

**0.0**   Begin at the west end of the parking lot and stop at the bridge overlook.

**0.1**   Continue across the bridge and turn right.

**0.6**   Arrive at Farm Ford.

**1.0**   Arrive at the Van Pelt House Site.

**1.4**   Arrive back at the parking lot.

# 5 Brawner Farm

The area of this hike is on land that had been farmed since the Revolutionary War and continued until the twentieth century, including during the Second Battle of Bull Run, which took place here in August 1862.

**Main interest:** History

**Distance:** 2-mile loop

**Hiking time:** About 2 hours

**Difficulty:** Easy

**Trail surface:** Natural surfaces, mowed grass

**Best season:** Year-round; open fields can get hot in summer.

**Other trail users:** Runners, horses

**Canine compatibility:** Dogs allowed on leash

**Fees and permits:** None

**Schedule:** Daily dawn to dusk; Interpretive Center open daily 9 a.m. to 5 p.m.

**Facilities:** None

**Map:** www.nps.gov/mana/plan yourvisit/maps.htm

**Trail contact:** Manassas National Battlefield Park, 12521 Lee Hwy., Manassas 20109; (703) 361-1339; www.nps.gov/mana/index .htm

**Finding the Trailhead:** From I-66 West, take exit 43B onto US 29 North (Lee Highway). Keep right to stay on Lee Highway. In 1.2 miles, turn left on Pageland Lane; the parking area will be on your right. GPS: N38 48.802' / W77 33.923'

## The Hike

The original farm was purchased by a veteran of the Revolutionary War, George Tennille, as a new route to the port at the Potomac River was built, increasing the opportunity for trade. The farm was rented to the Brawner family a few years before the outbreak of the Civil War. The house that stands today is not the original, but archeologists have uncovered the foundation from 1800 and several artifacts that predate the Civil War. The farmhouse is now an interpretive center and should be the first stop before your hike.

Walking through the quiet open fields, it's hard to imagine General "Stonewall" Jackson standing here at the site of the opening battle of the Second Battle of Bull Run. The battle ended at nightfall but continued the next day at nearby Battery Heights, leading to a Confederate victory. As you walk, look for markers with quotes from soldiers who fought, and survived, here.

Walk from the parking lot through a small meadow and stop to look at the archeological dig site before entering the Brawner farmhouse. Rangers are available to answer questions, and a large map display tells the story of the fighting that took place around here. Take a look at the other exhibits, including a model of the uniform worn by the 5th New York Infantry Regiment, known as "Duryée's Zouaves." Abram Duryée was a Union general of French descent. Zouave uniforms consist of baggy pants, a vest and sash, and a fez-like hat. Elmer Ellsworth from New York adopted the style from the French army along with some of their drill practices and created the first Zouave Cadet team in 1859. By the time the Civil War began, there were about one hundred Zouave units, about seventy in the Union and twenty-five in the Confederacy.

Exit from the back of the farmhouse and bear left up to a small hill with Confederate cannons. These were used on the second day of fighting to hold off Union troops advancing from the east. From here, follow the mowed path east through the farm fields that, in spring and summer, are covered in wildflowers. The trail will turn right at the sign

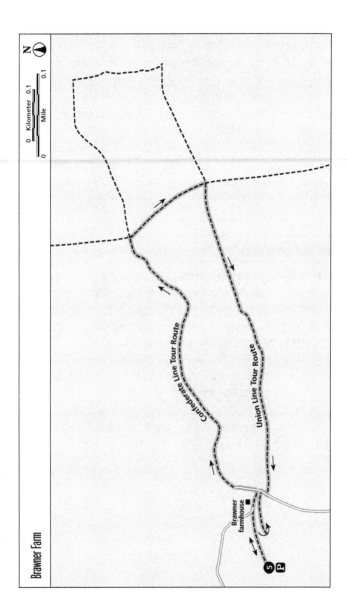

Brawner Farm

with a quote from Major A. A. Lowther of the 15th Alabama. Continue on the loop trail to the top of a small hill. You can see the farmhouse ahead, but take a minute to enjoy the view from here. There is a large shade tree with a bench—quite welcome if you're out on a hot day. Near the house is a group of historical markers about the battle that are worth reading. From there, continue back to the parking lot.

Tours are given of the battlefield; check the website for more information. The high grasses that parallel the trail are places where you might find ticks. Be sure to check for them after you hike. Also see the previous hikes for information on things to do in the area after your hike.

## Miles and Directions

**0.0** Begin at the east side of the parking lot and follow the walkway through the meadow to the archeological exhibit and the Brawner farmhouse.

**0.25** Exit the farmhouse on the east side and walk left up a short hill to the cannons. Then continue east along the trail.

**0.75** The trail comes to an intersection at the sign with the quote from the Confederate soldier. Turn right and follow the trail as it goes straight and then bears right.

**1.75** Stop at the bench just before reaching the farmhouse. Then continue back to the farmhouse and return to the parking lot.

**2.0** Arrive back at the parking lot.

# 6 Prince William Forest

Experience a taste of this national park with its fascinating history and serene beauty, just a short 45-minute drive from Washington, D.C.

**Main interest:** Nature, wildlife, history

**Distance:** 1-mile loop

**Hiking time:** About 1 hour

**Difficulty:** Easy

**Trail surface:** Natural surfaces

**Best season:** Year-round, especially beautiful in fall

**Other trail users:** None

**Canine compatibility:** Dogs allowed on leash

**Fees and permits:** $15 per vehicle

**Schedule:** Daily dawn to dusk

**Facilities:** Restrooms

**Map:** www.nps.gov/prwi/plan yourvisit/maps.htm

**Trail contact:** Prince William Forest Park, 18170 Park Entrance Rd., Triangle 22172; (703) 221-7181; www.nps.gov/prwi/index .htm

**Finding the Trailhead:** From I-95 South, take exit 150B onto VA 619/Joplin Road. Take the second right at Park Entrance Road into the park. From there, follow the signs to the Oak Ridge Campground parking lot. GPS: N38 5852' / W77 3947'

## The Hike

The land that makes up Prince William Forest Park was primarily farmland and two communities of freed slaves known as Batestown and Hickory Ridge. Many residents worked at the Cabin Branch Pyrite Mine, also located in what is now the park. The mine was open from 1889 to 1920, and the ruins can be seen on a short but difficult hike. The Washington-Rochambeau Revolutionary Route, which leads from Vermont to Yorktown, Virginia, crosses the park and can be seen on the Crossing Trail.

In the 1930s, the towns and the surrounding farms were asked to vacate under the authority of the Resettlement Administration, part of Roosevelt's New Deal, whose goal was to create new parks and several summer camps for city kids. The local residents, however, refused to move until they were forced out when the area was taken over during World War II and used by the Office of Strategic Services (OSS) to train spies. After the war, the land was given to the National Park Service and is the largest protected natural area in the Washington Metro area.

This hike goes through an area that was farmland only eighty years ago, but the forest has completely reclaimed the land. Because the park is located between the northern and southern regions, several species of trees are able to survive. The forest is the largest national park in the Piedmont region. The ground is covered with ground cedar, a native plant, and above are red maples, dogwoods, poplars, oaks, and pine trees. Birds in the area include warblers and hawks, and look for foxes and deer as well.

The hike begins at the Oak Ridge Campground. Look for yellow and green blazes at the trailhead. Very soon after starting, the trail comes to a fork. Bear right and continue to the intersection with the Farms to Forest Trail Loop. Follow the trail straight ahead to finish the loop back to the parking area.

The park has several other hikes if you have the time. When you enter the park and drive to the Oak Ridge Campground, you will take the Scenic Drive to its halfway point. When you leave, drive the other direction to experience more of this beautiful park and its history.

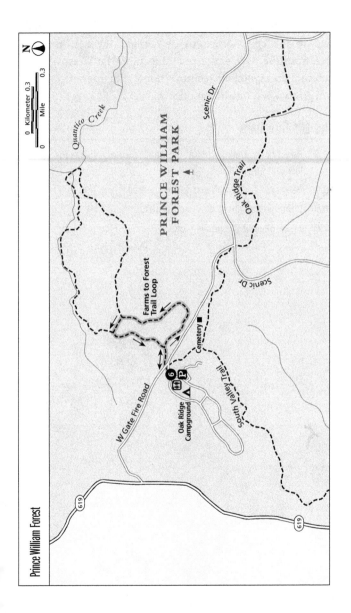

Prince William Forest

Nearby is the town of Dumfries, the oldest chartered town in the commonwealth of Virginia. It's a 10-minute drive from the park entrance and features the Weems-Botts Museum, an eighteenth-century home. For more information, go to www.historicdumfriesva.org/.

## Miles and Directions

**0.0** Begin at the trailhead from the parking lot and follow the yellow and green blazes.

**0.1** Bear right at the fork and follow the trail.

**0.5** Continue straight to stay on this trail.

**1.0** Arrive back at the parking lot.

# 7 Bull Run Bluebell Trail

Mark your calendar for April to experience the bluebell fields at Bull Run Park. Nothing compares to the amazing sight of this huge blanket of blue.

**Main interest:** Nature, wildflowers
**Distance:** 1.5-mile loop
**Hiking time:** About 2 hours
**Difficulty:** Easy
**Trail surface:** Natural surfaces
**Best season:** Year-round; late March to mid-April for the bluebells
**Other trail users:** Runners
**Canine compatibility:** Dogs allowed on leash
**Fees and permits:** No fee for residents of Fairfax, Arlington, Prince William, and Loudoun Counties; $8 per car for others
**Schedule:** Daily dawn to dusk
**Facilities:** Restrooms, picnic area
**Map:** www.novaparks.com/sites/default/files/maps/Bull%20Run%20Park%20Map_0.pdf
**Trail contact:** Bull Run Regional Park, 7700 Bull Run Dr., Centreville 20121; (703) 631-0550; www.novaparks.com/parks/bull-run-regional-park/things-to-do/bluebell-trail

**Finding the Trailhead:** From I-66 West, take exit 52 onto US 29 (Lee Highway) toward Centreville. In 2.5 miles, turn left on Bull Run Post Office Road. In about 1 mile, as the road curves to the left, turn right onto Bull Run Drive. The park entrance is about 2 miles ahead. Park in the lot by the campground. GPS: N38 7960' / W77 4361'

## The Hike

Spring in the Washington, D.C., region is perhaps best known for its explosion of pink cherry trees, most famously by the Tidal Basin, but they actually bloom all over the region. A lesser-known gem of springtime in the area are the bluebells that also are abundant in the region. The largest group of bluebells on the East Coast can be found in Bull Run Regional Park from the end of March to mid-April along this trail. The flowers like damp soil, and the Bull Run floodplain provides the perfect environment for them to spread out over the forest floor. If you go earlier in bluebell season, you might see the hot pink buds before they open; a little later they open up partially to a blue-violet color. The peak color is a medium blue that carpets the forest floor and usually occurs in mid-April, but you can call the park or visit the website for an update each year. At any stage, the bluebells are spectacular, but the peak blossom time is truly magical. The plant goes dormant once the trees, many dogwoods and maples, fill out in early summer. The trail goes past Bull Run and can, at times, become muddy.

While the spring bluebells bloom is naturally the best time to hike this trail, it's a nice walk any time of the year just to get into the woods and away from the nearby city. The park has lots of other amenities, including other hiking trails, picnic areas, Frisbee golf, a playground, and the Atlantis Waterpark. The Bull Run Festival of Lights, open from Thanksgiving to New Year's Day, is a popular drive through a festive light display ending at a holiday village.

Less than 30 minutes from Bull Run Regional Park is the town of Clifton, a charming small town. The main street has several historic homes, including one that belonged to a passenger on the *Titanic*. The Orange and Alexandria Railroad went through here, a crucial transportation route during the Civil War. The town has restaurants and a wonderful ice cream place. Fairfax County's first winery is nearby as well. More information can be found at www.fxva.com/neighborhoods/clifton/explore-clifton/.

# Bull Run Bluebell Trail

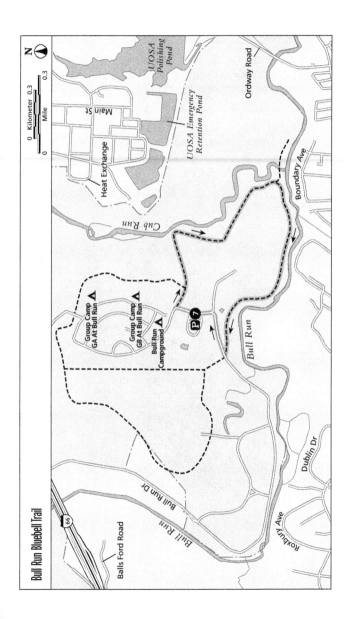

# Miles and Directions

**0.0** Walk across from the parking lot, away from the picnic shelters, and follow the sign for the Bluebell Trail. The trail is clearly marked and goes around in a loop.

**1.5** Exit the woods and arrive back by the picnic shelters and parking lot.

# 8 Difficult Run Stream Valley Trail

Explore a portion of this amazing county connector trail that winds through busy Fairfax County and highlights many natural preservation spaces.

**Main interest:** Nature, wildlife, bird watching

**Distance:** 4.2 miles out and back

**Hiking time:** About 3 hours

**Difficulty:** Easy to moderate

**Trail surface:** Natural and paved surfaces

**Best season:** Year-round; can be icy on very cold winter days

**Other trail users:** Runners, mountain bikers

**Canine compatibility:** Dogs allowed on leash

**Fees and permits:** None

**Schedule:** Daily dawn to dusk

**Facilities:** None

**Map:** www.fairfaxcounty.gov/ parks/sites/parks/files/assets/ documents/trails/cct-9-difficult -run-stream-valley.pdf

**Trail contact:** Fairfax County Park Authority, 12055 Government Center Pkwy., Fairfax 22035; (703) 324-8702; www .fairfaxcounty.gov/parks/trails/ cross-county-trail

**Finding the Trailhead:** From I-66 West, take exit 60 (VA 123 North) toward Vienna. Turn left onto Jermantown Road and after almost 1 mile, turn right into the Oak Marr RECenter parking lot. GPS: N38 8752' / W77 3158'

## The Hike

Difficult Run Stream Valley Trail is part of the Gerry Connolly Cross County trail system, named for the US congressman who represents this region. The trail stretches for more than 40 miles from close to Great Falls National Park south to the Occoquan River. Difficult Run is a 15.9-mile creek that eventually flows into the Potomac River. The stream and its tributaries make up the largest watershed in Fairfax County. The cross county trail has two sections named for this waterway. This hike covers a portion of the trail that is farther inland in the residential towns of Oakton and Vienna.

This hike begins by walking from the Oak Marr parking lot back out to Jermantown Road. Turn left and the trailhead is on the left just past the recreation center building. You'll enter the woods, and after about 0.3 mile, the trail turns left and crosses Difficult Run before bearing right and paralleling the stream up to Miller Heights Road. Look for deer, which are all over this park, and, if you're lucky, you might see a beaver in the stream. The trail is also popular for birding, especially during the spring and fall migration months when many species can be heard and may be seen, including hawks, flycatchers, and blackbirds. When you reach Miller Heights Road, turn around and return by the same route.

The trailhead for this hike is in Oakton, Virginia, which is in between the town of Vienna and the city of Fairfax, both interesting places to visit. Vienna has lots of restaurants, and the Washington and Old Dominion rails-to-trails route passes through. A small park has an original caboose and rail station from the 1920s. Fairfax is the county seat, but the Old Town section also has restaurants and shops. Both towns are about 3 miles from the trail. For more information, visit www.viennava.gov/ and www.fairfaxva.gov/.

## Miles and Directions

**0.0**   Begin at the Oak Marr RECenter parking lot, walk back out to Jermantown Road, and turn left.

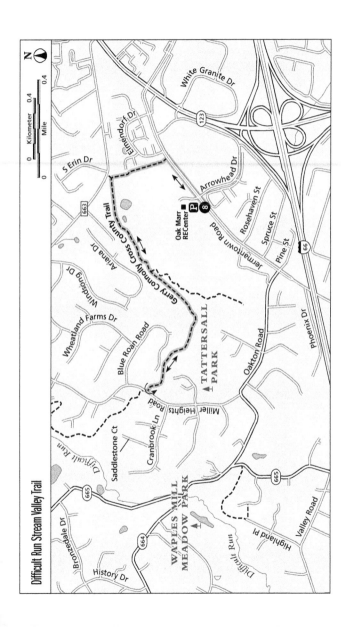

Difficult Run Stream Valley Trail

N

0       0.4
Kilometer

0       0.4
Mile

White Granite Dr

S Erin Dr

Elmendorf Dr

123

Arrowhead Dr

Oak Marr
RECenter

P

8

Jermantown Road

Rosehaven St

Spruce St

Pine St

66

663

Ariana Dr

Windsong Dr

Gerry Connolly Cross County Trail

Wheatland Farms Dr

Blue Roan Road

▲ TATTERSALL PARK

Miller Heights Road

Oakton Road

Phoenix Dr

Difficult Run

Saddlestone Ct

Cranbrook Ln

665

WAPLES MILL MEADOW PARK

664

Bronzedale Dr

History Dr

Difficult Run

Highland Pl

Valley Road

665

**0.3** Turn left onto the trail.

**0.6** Turn left to continue on the trail.

**2.1** At Miller Heights Road, turn around and return on the same route.

**4.2** Arrive back at the parking lot.

# 9 Fountainhead Trail

This is a beautiful hike through a forest of pine trees and two historic cemeteries.

**Main interest:** Nature, history

**Distance:** 4 miles out and back

**Hiking time:** About 3 hours

**Difficulty:** Easy to moderate

**Trail surface:** Natural surfaces

**Best season:** Year-round; fall is great for foliage.

**Other trail users:** Runners, cyclists, horses

**Canine compatibility:** Dogs allowed on leash

**Fees and permits:** None

**Schedule:** Daily dawn to dusk

**Facilities:** Restrooms (may be closed in the off-season)

**Map:** www.novaparks.com/sites/default/files/styles/full_width/public/maps/BROT%20horizontal%20web.jpg?itok=ANXF_O-x

**Trail contact:** Fountainhead Regional Park, 10875 Hampton Rd., Fairfax Station 22039; (703) 250-9124; www.novaparks.com/parks/fountainhead-regional-park

**Finding the Trailhead:** From I-66 West, take exit 55 onto VA 286 South (Fairfax County Parkway). After about 7 miles, merge onto Ox Road South. In 3 miles, turn right on Henderson Road/VA 643, then in 2 miles turn left on Hampton Road/VA 647. The park entrance is about 1.5 miles ahead on the right. Park in the first parking lot on the right. GPS: N38 7274' / W77 3232'

## The Hike

Fountainhead Park is at one end of the 19-mile Bull Run Occoquan Trail, a National Recreation Trail that connects this park with Bull Run and meanders through woods, past streams, and up and down hills. The park is overseen by the Northern Virginia Regional Park Authority, which ensures the area's flora and fauna are protected. The trail is maintained by the Potomac Appalachian Trail Club.

The main feature of this park is the lake, which was created by a dam on the Occoquan River and is popular for kayaking, canoeing, and fishing; it also provides drinking water for much of Fairfax County. The trail begins by the parking lot and right at the beginning is the Davis Lewis Cemetery. Not much is known about these families, but most of the graves are from the nineteenth and early twentieth centuries, meaning they probably lived in this area when it was much less developed.

The trail is well-marked with blue blazes and continues up and down through the forest of pine, beech, and hemlock trees, among many others. In springtime, look for flowering dogwoods, the state tree and flower of Virginia. Animals in the area include deer, rabbits, bald eagles, and wild turkeys.

After about 2 miles, you will cross Wolf Run Shoals Road and arrive at the Fairfax Buckley Cemetery. The graves include those of four people who died in 1918, presumably from the Spanish flu, and Wellington Fairfax, a veteran of the Confederate army. Near here is a marker showing that this was part of the Washington-Rochambeau Revolutionary Route. This route extends for more than 600 miles and was traveled by the Continental and French armies in 1781 from New England to Yorktown, where they defeated the British in the Revolutionary War.

From this point, turn around and return the way you came.

After your hike, you might want to get out on the beautiful Fountainhead Lake. It's a short drive to the marina; just continue on Hampton Road for about 1 mile. The marina rents kayaks, canoes, and jon boats from April through

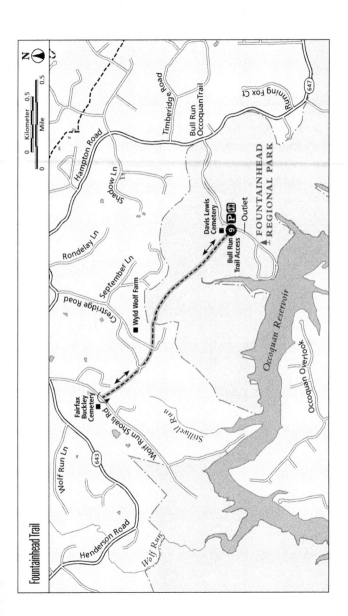

Fountainhead Trail

November. There are restrooms open year-round here as well. Hours vary depending on the season, so please check the website.

## Miles and Directions

**0.0** Begin at the trailhead by the parking lot.

**0.1** Make a stop at the Davis Lewis Cemetery.

**2.0** Cross Wolf Shoals Run Road to the Fairfax Buckley Cemetery and then turn around.

**4.0** Arrive back at the parking lot.

# 10  Winkler Botanical Preserve

A sanctuary lies in the midst of office and condo buildings in one of the busiest suburbs in the Metro region. Escape and rejuvenate on this short nature hike.

**Main interest:** Nature

**Distance:** 1 mile out and back

**Hiking time:** About 1 hour

**Difficulty:** Easy

**Trail surface:** Natural surfaces

**Best season:** Year-round

**Other trail users:** None

**Canine compatibility:** Dogs not allowed

**Fees and permits:** None

**Schedule:** Daily 8:30 a.m. to 4 p.m.; closed on major holidays

**Facilities:** None

**Map:** www.alltrails.com/explore/trail/us/virginia/winkler-botanical-preserve-trail?ref=sidebar-view-full-map

**Trail contact:** Winkler Botanical Preserve, 5400 Roanoke Ave., Alexandria 22311; (703) 578-7888

**Finding the Trailhead:** From I-495 South, merge onto I-395 North toward Washington. Take exit 3A onto VA 236 (Duke Street). In 0.5 mile, keep right and then turn left on South Van Dorn Street. In 1 mile turn left on Sanger Avenue, then right on Sheffield Court, and right on Roanoke Avenue. The entrance is ahead past the apartment building. Drive through the gate; there are parking spots on the left. GPS: N38 49.660' / W77 07.404'

## The Hike

The land that now incorporates the Winkler Botanical Preserve was once an abandoned pig farm that then became a dump. The Winkler family purchased the land in the 1980s and had a vision to create a nature preserve in the middle of a commercial and industrial area of Alexandria. They redirected three local streams to feed into a lake that is the central point of the park. A waterfall cascades on one side, and on the other is the Catherine Lodge, used primarily for nature education for local schoolchildren. The preserve features native plants and trees that attract a lot of wildlife, including geese, deer, and foxes.

In 2010, part of the 44 acres was threatened with destruction by a federal government act that would have constructed an off-ramp from I-395 into the park. The people of Alexandria, led by the children, campaigned to fight it—and they won. A seventh-grade class prepared an environmental assessment outlining the impacts the project would have on the remaining areas of the park's wildlife, water, and air. Every elementary school child in the city of Alexandria has been on at least one field trip to the Winkler Botanical Preserve. The programs that are offered focus on environmental preservation and protection, and they teach kids how animals survive and how plants grow. It is a treasured oasis in the middle of the busy I-395 corridor.

After parking, walk straight until you reach the lodge and lake. Directly across is the two-tiered waterfall, and you will likely see geese swimming in the water. From there continue straight on the path, crossing the stream on the stepping stones. After passing over the stream, turn right and follow the path bearing left to a wooden bridge. Cross over for a nice view of the lake. You can walk up the path a bit farther above the falls, but beware that geese are often hanging out here and might impede you by honking and getting in your way! Turn around and return across the bridge to the path, to the lodge, and back down the road to the parking area.

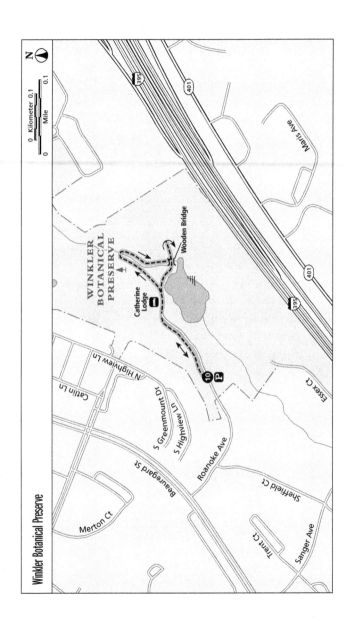

Winkler Botanical Preserve

The preserve is in a busy part of Alexandria, but only a 30-minute drive away is Old Town Alexandria with its cobblestone streets, many historic sites, and multitude of shops and restaurants. The town dates back to the 1600s and was frequented by George Washington and other patriots. It sits along the Potomac River between Washington, D.C., and Mount Vernon. Some famous spots are Christ Church, Gatsby's Tavern, and the Robert E. Lee's Boyhood Home. The Saturday farmers' market has been operating continually for more than 250 years. Find out more at www.visit alexandriava.com/.

## Miles and Directions

**0.0**   Begin at the parking area and walk up the road into the park.

**0.2**   Arrive at the lodge and the lake. Follow the path straight ahead and then cross the stream.

**0.4**   After crossing the stream, turn right and follow the path bearing left to the wooden bridge.

**0.6**   Turn around and follow the path with the lake on your left.

**1.0**   Arrive back at the parking area.

# 11 Burke Lake

Voted one of the ten best fitness trails in the country, Burke Lake is very popular with local residents for hiking and lots of family activities as well.

**Main interest:** Nature, bird watching
**Distance:** 4.7-mile loop
**Hiking time:** About 2.5 hours
**Difficulty:** Easy
**Trail surface:** Gravel and natural surfaces
**Best season:** Year-round
**Other trail users:** Runners, cyclists
**Canine compatibility:** Dogs allowed on leash
**Fees and permits:** No fee for Fairfax County residents; on weekends and holidays, nonresidents are charged $10 per car.

**Schedule:** Mon to Fri 8 a.m. to 6 p.m.; Sat and Sun 6 a.m. to 6 p.m.
**Facilities:** Restrooms, drinking water, picnic tables, snack bar (check website for hours)
**Map:** www.fairfaxcounty.gov/ parks/sites/parks/files/ assets/documents/waterfront/ burkelake/burketrailmap.pdf
**Trail contact:** Burke Lake Park, 7315 Ox Rd., Fairfax Station 22039; (703) 323-6600; www.fairfaxcounty.gov/parks/ burke-lake

**Finding the Trailhead:** From I-66 West, take exit 55 onto VA 286 South (Fairfax County Parkway). After about 7 miles, merge onto Ox Road/VA 123 South. After about 2 miles, the entrance will be on your left. Follow the signs for the marina and park there. GPS: N38 7616' / W77 3041'

# The Hike

Burke Lake was created when a dam was built on South Run, a tributary of the Potomac River. There is a park with a carousel and a kids' train, miniature golf, and playgrounds, but the main feature here is the lake. Used for boating and fishing, the 218-acre lake is also home to more than 200 species of birds, including herons, egrets, and loons. Cardinals, the state bird of Virginia, are often seen here, and, in winter, their bright red color is quite remarkable. Swimming is not allowed in the lake.

The trailhead is near the parking area to the west near the disc golf field. The trail follows the lake edge most of the way. Follow the path past the carousel and amphitheater. It will wind around the west end of the lake and then pass a campground before heading up and around the northern arm. At about mile 3, look for Vesper Island, a state waterfowl refuge. After 3.5 miles, you'll cross the dam that formed the lake before returning back to the marina. Along the way, look for wildlife such as deer and common black snakes, which are harmless.

The trail can get busy on the weekends, especially in spring and fall when the weather is good. Keep an eye out for cyclists and runners.

There are great amenities for kids, like the carousel and train, and the park offers many special events throughout the year, such as birding boat tours and Halloween train rides. Check the website for operating hours and dates. In winter, most of the other attractions are closed, making it a great time to focus on the natural beauty.

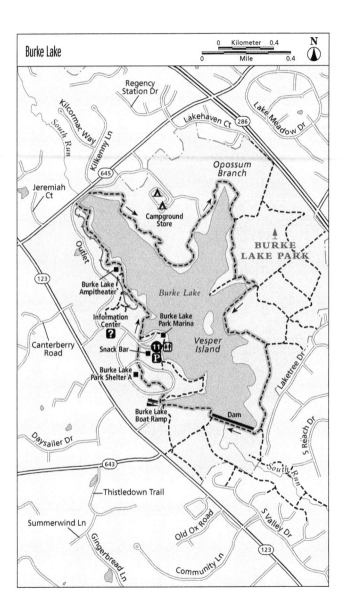

# Miles and Directions

**0.0**  Begin at the trailhead near the marina parking lot.

**0.9**  The trail veers right past the amphitheater to continue around the lake.

**2.3**  Bear right to stay on the trail as it turns around the inlet.

**3.0**  Pass Vesper Island.

**3.7**  Cross the dam and continue straight back to the parking lot.

**4.7**  Arrive back at the parking lot.

# 12 Meadowlark Gardens

See native plants, wetlands, a bell of peace, and much more on this delightful walk through the gardens.

**Main interest:** Gardens
**Distance:** 1.6-mile loop
**Hiking time:** About 2 hours
**Difficulty:** Easy
**Trail surface:** Paved and mulch surfaces
**Best season:** Year-round
**Other trail users:** None
**Canine compatibility:** Dogs not allowed
**Fees and permits:** $6 per person
**Schedule:** Open daily at 10 a.m.; closing hours vary by season; closed Thanksgiving, Christmas, and New Year's Days and if

weather conditions are prohibitive to walking
**Facilities:** Restrooms, drinking water, nature center, gift shop
**Maps:** www.novaparks.com/ sites/default/files/maps/MeadowlarkMap.pdf; maps also available at the visitor center.
**Trail contact:** Meadowlark Botanical Gardens, 9750 Meadowlark Gardens Ct., Vienna 22182; (703) 255-3631; www.novaparks.com/parks/ meadowlark-botanical-gardens

**Finding the Trailhead:** From I-495 North, take exit 46A onto VA 123 South toward Tysons Corner. In 1.5 miles, turn right on Old Courthouse Road, and then immediately left again to stay on Old Courthouse Road. This road changes its name to Beulah Road NE. In about 3 miles, turn left into the parking lot. GPS: N38 9384' / W77 2812'

## The Hike

Meadowlark Botanical Gardens is a 95–acre garden featuring native plants, including azaleas, dogwoods, crape myrtles; aquatic plants; and an herb collection. There is a large pond with a dock and gazebo, a great meadow, and a children's tea garden. There is something to see year-round, but highlights are the azaleas and cherry trees in spring, crape myrtles in late summer, and a winter wonderland walk in December and January.

The gardens are operated by the Northern Virginia Regional Park Authority and are preserved for conservation, education, and community. Regardless of the time of year, it's always a serene haven in which to escape the frenzy of city life.

Begin at the visitor center, where there are displays and other information and a small gift shop. As you exit the building out the back, bear left and walk past the picnic area to the crape myrtle and crab-apple gardens. The crab apples bloom in spring in shades from light to dark pink and produce yellow and red leaves in the fall. Crape myrtles flower in July and come in colors including purple, pink, and maroon. Return toward the picnic area and bear left past the lilacs and then right to the gazebo, where many colors of azaleas bloom in the spring. From here, follow the mulch path until it rejoins the paved walk and turn right. Follow the spiral path on your right to get a nice view of the gardens and the lake. Return to the path and continue through the tea garden and then slightly left to cross the small pond. Continue straight across the path onto the trail that heads into the woods. Follow this until it loops back and pass a small Virginia native wetland garden on your left. Rejoin the paved path to the lake and walk out onto the dock. Look for large koi fish and turtles from the dock. Go back to the paved trail and turn right and then left to visit the Korean Bell Garden. The Bell of Peace and Harmony symbolizes the friendship between the United States and South Korea and is engraved with symbols of longevity, the rose of Sharon (representing South Korea), and the dogwood (representing Virginia).

# Meadowlark Gardens

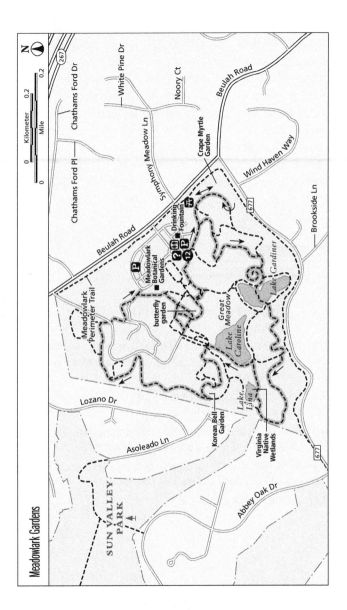

Continue past the bell, turn right on the path, and walk past native Virginia trees and shrubs. Follow the path back toward the visitor center, but turn right and detour to the butterfly garden. From there, follow the path that runs along the Great Meadow and then left back to the entrance.

The distance of this hike varies because there are so many small extensions into gardens throughout this park. Explore any or all that interest you.

Just 3 miles from here is downtown Vienna, with lots of places to eat and drink. Check out historic Church Street and the nearby Town Square Park. For more information, see www.viennava.gov/.

## Miles and Directions

**0.0**   Begin at the visitor center. Turn left to the Crape Myrtle Garden.

**0.1**   Return to the first intersection and go left to the spiral path and walk to the top.

**0.2**   Follow the path across the pond and onto the trail into the woods. Follow this as it loops around past the wetland and rejoins the path.

**0.6**   Walk onto the dock. Return to the path and follow it right then left to the Korean Bell.

**0.9**   Continue on the path as it winds around the gardens and loops back past a log cabin and the visitor center.

**1.4**   Go straight ahead to the butterfly garden before turning around and returning to the visitor center.

**1.6**   Arrive back at the visitor center.

# 13 Rust Nature Sanctuary

Look for bluebirds, frogs, turtles, and deer on this venture into nature.

**Main interest:** Nature, birds, wildlife

**Distance:** 1-mile loop

**Hiking time:** About 1 hour

**Difficulty:** Easy

**Trail surface:** Natural and paved surfaces

**Best season:** Year-round

**Other trail users:** None

**Canine compatibility:** Dogs allowed on leash

**Fees and permits:** None

**Schedule:** Daily dawn to dusk

**Facilities:** Restrooms, picnic tables

**Map:** www.novaparks.com/sites/default/files/maps/Rust%20Map%201-17%20Final.pdf

**Trail contact:** Rust Nature Sanctuary, 802 Children's Center Rd., Leesburg 20175; (703) 669-0755; www.novaparks.com/parks/rust-sanctuary

**Finding the Trailhead:** From VA 7 West, merge onto US 15 South toward Winchester. In 2 miles, exit at US 15 Business to Leesburg. In 0.5 mile, turn left on Catoctin Circle and then in 1 mile turn left onto Childrens Center Road. Follow this to the sign for Rust Manor House. Continue up the hill and enter the park through a stone gate. The parking lot is directly ahead. GPS: N38 07.187' / W77 35.307'

## The Hike

This nature sanctuary is part of the Virginia Bird and Wildlife Trail. The property and the hundred-year-old Rust Manor were donated to the Audubon Naturalist Society by the heirs of Margaret Rust, who wished that the property remain undeveloped as a nature preserve. She wrote, "This is a beautiful, unique and well-balanced habitat that I would like to save as a refuge for all types of wildlife, as it is now, and I earnestly believe, should remain." The park is run by a partnership between the Northern Virginia (NOVA) Park Authority and the Audubon Naturalist Society. They offer educational nature programs, and the manor house is open for special events, weddings in particular.

As you take the hike, you will notice several bluebird nesting boxes provided by the Virginia Bluebird Society. Bluebirds are one of the many bird species that nest in cavities, and their numbers are declining in the United States, mainly due to urban development. These wooden boxes are set out for the bluebirds to nest. Volunteers do bird counts from April to August and record their nests, hatched eggs, and fledglings and send the data to the Virginia Bluebird Society.

Start the hike at the Rust Manor and walk to the left side to the Pollinator Garden. On the left is the beginning of the Pollinator Garden Trail. Take this for just a short walk and then keep right to continue on the trail to the pond. Listen for the familiar sound of frogs and look for turtles as you walk past the pond and up a paved road to the entrance to the Oak Trail. This takes you through a small forest before connecting with the Meadow Loop Trail. The trail here is mowed grass and fields of flowers. Turn right and follow the loop until you see a fork and a sign on the right pointing to the vernal pool. The trail narrows here as you walk down to the pool. A vernal pool is a place where water collects, usually in spring, and stays long enough to create an ecosystem. Vernal pools are necessary for certain species to survive. They provide a safe breeding ground for many amphibians, including frogs, where they won't be taken over by fish. Native

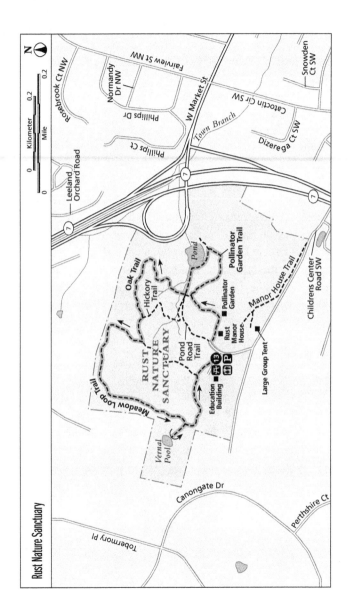

Rust Nature Sanctuary

plants also thrive in a vernal pool because of the nutrient richness of the water and soil. Loudoun County has worked hard to preserve many vernal pools, and this one is a great example.

From the vernal pool, return to the main trail and continue until you see the maintenance shed and large opening in the foliage. Go through this and you will be in the outdoor classroom area; the picnic area and parking lot are just ahead.

The old town section of Leesburg is about a 5-minute drive away. Stop there for a bite to eat or have a look in the many antiques stores. Or sample a local brew at one of the new brewpubs that have opened up in recent years. If you'd like to stay longer in the countryside, there are several wineries nearby; the ones closest to Rust Sanctuary are on the Loudoun Heights Cluster. Check the website: www.visit loudoun.org/drink/wine-country/clusters/. There is also information on breweries in the region.

## Miles and Directions

**0.0** Begin by walking on the left side of the manor house to the back to the Pollinator Garden. Join the trail there and bear right to walk to the pond.

**0.2** Walk up the paved road to the entrance to the Oak Trail.

**0.4** From the Oak Trail, turn right onto the Meadow Loop Trail.

**0.7** Turn right to visit the vernal pool.

**1.0** Arrive back at the parking lot.

# 14  Huntley Meadows Park

The early mornings and the evenings showcase an abundance of aquatic birds and other wildlife in this wetland park.

**Main interest:** Bird watching, wildlife

**Distance:** 1.9-mile lollipop

**Hiking time:** About 1.5 hours

**Difficulty:** Easy

**Trail surface:** Natural surface, boardwalk

**Best season:** Year-round

**Other trail users:** None

**Canine compatibility:** Dogs not allowed on the boardwalk

**Fees and permits:** None

**Schedule:** Daily dawn to dusk; visitor center hours vary.

**Facilities:** Restrooms, drinking water (when visitor center is open)

**Map:** www.fairfaxcounty.gov/ parks/huntley-meadows/map

**Trail contact:** Huntley Meadows Park, 3701 Lockheed Blvd., Alexandria 22306; (703) 768-2525; www.fairfaxcounty.gov/parks/ huntley-meadows

**Finding the Trailhead:** From I-495, take exit 173 onto Van Dorn Street toward Franconia. Turn left on South Van Dorn Street, then make an immediate left on Telegraph Road and a right on South Kings Highway. Turn right on Harrison Lane and bear slightly right at the intersection with Lockheed Boulevard and straight into the parking lot. GPS: N38 45.446' /W77 05.886'

## The Hike

The main feature of this hike is the vast nontidal wetland, the largest in Northern Virginia. This emergent marsh was created by a beaver dam in a low-lying floodplain of the Potomac River. In the 1980s, the marsh began to decline due to construction in the area and the spread of aggressive plants.

Studies were conducted in cooperation with the NOVA Park Authority to determine the best way to revitalize the wetland. In 2014, the restoration was completed. The project included creating a water-control system, deeper pools for aquatic life, and other areas to attract wildlife.

The land was originally owned by the George Mason family until the early 1900s, when it was sold off into smaller farms. For a brief time in the 1920s, several farms were purchased in hopes of creating a large airport. After this unsuccessful attempt, the land was bought by the federal government and used for various purposes, including military training. In 1975, it was donated to Fairfax County and is now the largest park run by the county authority. The park schedules several special tours throughout the year for both kids and adults, including sunset walks, stargazing events, and opportunities to learn about the ecosystem.

The hike begins in the woods near the Norma Hoffman Visitor Center, named for a champion of the park and the environment. From there it eventually opens out onto the boardwalk that expands over the marsh. Listen for frogs and look for turtles and ducks as you walk along. On the far side of the boardwalk is an observation tower near the beaver dam. There are more than 200 species of birds within the park. Great blue herons and egrets are easy to spot, but look also for sandpipers and woodpeckers.

The park includes Historic Huntley house, which was owned by Thomas Mason, the grandson of George Mason and a mayor of Alexandria. The almost 200-year-old house was used as a summer place, a farm, and a headquarters for Union troops during the Civil War. The Fairfax County Park Authority acquired the house and land, and it is used now for special events, and tours are offered on Saturday from April

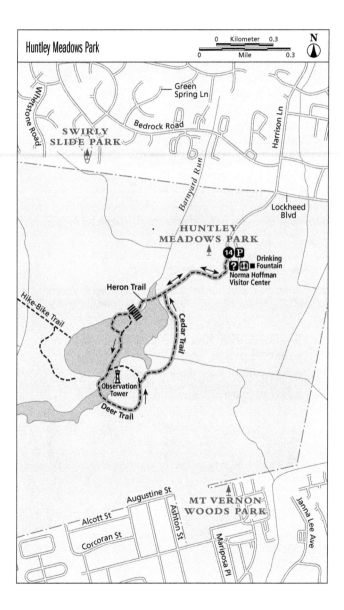

through October. The grounds are open daily dawn to dusk and are about a 1-mile walk in each direction from opposite sides of the parking lot, or a 2-minute drive.

Huntley Meadows is very close to both George Washington's home at Mount Vernon and Old Town Alexandria. If you want to see more wetlands, Dyke Marsh at Belle Haven isn't far either. Visit www.mountvernon.org, www.visit alexandriava.com, and www.nps.gov/gwmp/planyourvisit/dykemarsh.htm for more information.

## Miles and Directions

**0.0** Begin by accessing the trail from the parking lot by the sign for the visitor center.

**0.1** Bear right onto the boardwalk and continue to the right when the boardwalk comes to a fork.

**0.7** Climb the observation tower to get a better view of the wetlands and wildlife. Then continue on the boardwalk until it ends and the Deer Trail heads into the woods.

**1.1** Bear right onto the Cedar Trail and back to the intersection where the boardwalk began.

**1.8** Continue straight back toward the visitor center.

**1.9** Arrive back at the parking lot.

# 15 Silver Lake

This small park, with its peaceful lake and surroundings, is a perfect getaway. Do this quick, easy hike and bring a picnic to enjoy afterward.

**Main interest:** Nature, bird watching
**Distance:** 1.2-mile loop
**Hiking time:** About 1.5 hours
**Difficulty:** Easy
**Trail surface:** Natural, pebble, and paved surfaces
**Best season:** Year-round
**Other trail users:** Runners, horses
**Canine compatibility:** Dogs allowed on leash

**Fees and permits:** None
**Schedule:** Daily dawn to dusk
**Facilities:** Restrooms on the opposite side of the lake, picnic tables
**Map:** www.visitpwc.com/listing/silver-lake-park/460/
**Trail contact:** Silver Lake Park, 16198 Silver Lake Rd., Haymarket 20169; (703) 792-6000; www.visitpwc.com/listing/silver-lake-park/460/

**Finding the Trailhead:** From I-66 West, take exit 40 onto US 15 toward Haymarket. At the exit, turn left onto US 15 (James Madison Highway). In 0.5 mile, turn right on John Marshall Highway, and in 1 mile turn right on Antioch Road. Take this to Silver Lake Road and turn right. Follow the road past the equestrian center and turn left just after that. This road leads to the lake and parking lot. GPS: N38 52.962' / W77 17.944'

## The Hike

This small lake was created by nearby Bull Run and provides a quiet spot for an easy hike and bird watching. The area has lots of picnic spots, and fishing and kayaking are very popular as well. Begin the hike at the opposite side of the parking lot from the lake, where an opening in the bushes leads to a pebbled trail. Follow this until it intersects with a grass trail and then bear right. Continue as the trail surface changes to a gravel-dirt path. Pass by a field on the left that might have grazing horses; a rehabilitative equestrian farm is adjacent to the park. The path continues through a field that in summer is covered with purple and yellow wildflowers. There is an old cemetery on the right, off the trail, that it is believed to have belonged to the Mount family. There is only one broken headstone left, but there are a few other small markers with that name. As you continue, soon you'll see the lake on the right, and then follow the path to go around to the other side, where there are restrooms. Take some time to explore the small creek, and walk across the grass to a lookout deck right on the lake. Snowy egrets and other waterbirds are all around this area. There is another parking lot here and the kayak launch area.

Continue across the grass field to the road and turn right. Walk along the road to the other side of the lake and turn right to cross the dam. Be careful if the stones are wet or if you're hiking in cold weather; if it seems too slippery, you can walk past the dam and to the right to rejoin the trail on the other side. There are a few places to turn in where there are benches for relaxing with a view of the water. Continue back to the parking lot.

Silver Lake is in Haymarket, established in 1799 as a small farming community, and it was almost completely destroyed during the Civil War. The town's museum is about a 10-minute drive; it exhibits the history of the town and holds various festivals throughout the year. More information can be found at www.townofhaymarket.org/museum. Less than

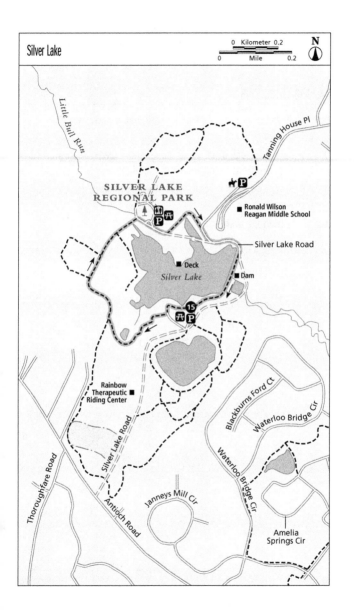

Silver Lake

0 Kilometer 0.2
0 Mile 0.2

N

Little Bull Run

Tanning House Pl

SILVER LAKE
REGIONAL PARK

Ronald Wilson
Reagan Middle School

Silver Lake Road

Deck

*Silver Lake*

Dam

15

Rainbow
Therapeutic
Riding Center

Blackburns Ford Ct

Waterloo Bridge Cir

Waterloo Bridge Cir

Thoroughfare Road

Silver Lake Road

Antioch Road

Janneys Mill Cir

Amelia
Springs Cir

30 minutes away is the town of Warrenton, a colonial trading center with a rich history. For information about Warrenton, go to www.warrentonva.gov/visitors.

## Miles and Directions

**0.0** Start the hike at the parking lot side that is away from the lakeshore.

**0.5** Stop at the deck overlooking the lake and creek. Then walk across the grass to the road and turn right.

**0.7** Turn right to cross over the dam. Turn right again to pick up the trail.

**1.2** Return to the parking lot.

# 16 Riverbend Park

This portion of the Potomac River is dotted with small islands and rocks and calm water, providing a serene approach to the Great Falls. Look for Canada geese, great blue herons, and, if you're lucky, a bald eagle.

**Main interest:** Nature, water, bird watching

**Distance:** 2.7 miles out and back

**Hiking time:** About 2 hours

**Difficulty:** Easy

**Trail surface:** Natural surface, some rougher terrain with rocks and tree roots

**Best season:** Year-round; parts of the trail can be icy in cold weather.

**Other trail users:** Horses on parts of the trail

**Canine compatibility:** Leashed dogs allowed

**Fees and permits:** None

**Schedule:** Daily 7 a.m. to dusk; visitor center hours vary, closed Tues

**Facilities:** Restrooms, drinking water, nature center, picnic tables

**Map:** www.fairfaxcounty.gov/parks/riverbend/trails

**Trail contact:** Riverbend Park, 8700 Potomac Hills St., Great Falls 22066; (703) 759-9018; www.fairfaxcounty.gov/parks/riverbend/

**Finding the Trailhead:** From VA 7 West, turn right on Springvale Road. In about 1.5 miles, turn right onto Georgetown Pike. In about 1 mile, turn left onto Walker Road and then right onto Arnon Chapel Road. In 1.5 miles, turn left onto River Bend Road, then immediately right on Jeffery Road, and right on Potomac Hills Street. Follow this to the end; the parking lot will be on your right. GPS: N39 01.054' / W77 14.771'

# The Hike

Make your first stop at the visitor center on the opposite side of the parking lot. There is a small nature exhibit, helpful staff, snacks for purchase, and restrooms. You can also pick up a map. From the visitor center, cross the parking lot, join the trail at the other end, and head south. The trail is part of the Potomac Heritage Trail that stretches for about 700 miles from Pennsylvania through Maryland, Virginia, and the District of Columbia and includes hiking, biking, and paddling routes. This section follows the Potomac River south to Great Falls National Park, with several beautiful spots for resting and enjoying the view. There are a few benches where you can stop and watch the river and birds. The park is a popular nesting place for migratory birds, and herons and egrets are often seen. There are also bald eagle nests around here, so keep an eye out for them. They are spectacular to see. In all, 191 species of birds have been spotted here.

After about 0.5 mile, look for Aqueduct Dam with its small waterfall that stretches across the river. This is what remains of an abandoned project to create a series of dams along the waterways of the Potomac Basin to provide water reservoirs and flood control and to control the water flow over Great Falls. The idea was born in the 1880s, but by 1969 it was terminated.

As you continue along the path, you can eventually hear the soft roar of Great Falls in the distance. Depending on the season, the trail is bordered with a variety of colorful wildflowers, such as asters and goldenrod. The flowers attract several butterflies, including monarchs, striped swallowtails, and blue brush-footeds. In spring, usually mid-March to

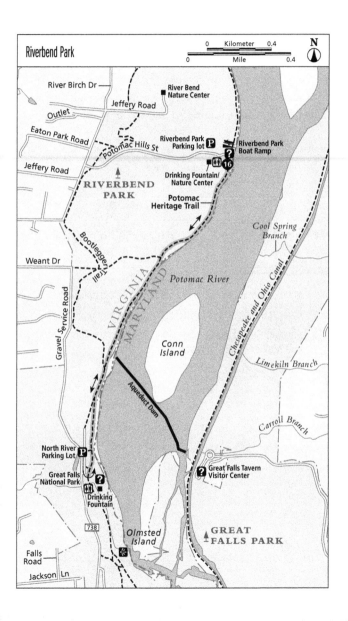

early April, the bluebells provide a spectacular scene. The park celebrates them with an annual festival.

As you enter Great Falls National Park, walk across the stone path and veer to the left to get a great view of the dam. Stop at the visitor center where there are nature and historic exhibits, information, and restrooms and other facilities. You might want to walk to the overlooks to see the falls before returning the same way back. Riverbend Park also offers special nature programs, wildlife viewing kayak tours, kayak rentals, and a boat launch.

The town of Great Falls is 10 minutes away and has a few restaurants, a pub, and a homemade ice cream shop. For more information, visit www.fxva.com/neighborhoods/great-falls.

## Miles and Directions

**0.0**  Begin at the trailhead on the south end of the parking lot.

**0.5**  Stop at the Aquaduct Dam. Then continue on the trail.

**1.4**  Arrive at Great Falls National Park Visitor Center. Turn around and return on the same trail.

**2.7**  Arrive back at the parking lot.

# 17 Neabsco Creek

This boardwalk hike crosses one of the first wetland mitigation projects in the United States. It was led by Julie Metz, an environmental scientist, for whom the wetlands are also named.

**Main interest:** Nature, bird watching, ecology
**Distance:** 1.5 miles out and back
**Hiking time:** About 1 hour
**Difficulty:** Easy
**Trail surface:** Boardwalk
**Best season:** Year-round; on hot summer days plan to visit early or late.
**Other trail users:** Runners, cyclists

**Canine compatibility:** Dogs allowed on leash
**Fees and permits:** None
**Schedule:** Daily dawn to dusk
**Map:** Not available.
**Trail contact:** Neabsco Creek Boardwalk, 15125 Blackburn Rd., Woodbridge 22191; www.pwcgov .org/government/dept/park/ neabsco/Pages/default.aspx

**Finding the Trailhead:** From I-495 South, take the exit to I-95 South toward Richmond. In 13 miles, take exit 156 toward Rippon Landing. In 0.5 mile, keep left toward VA 784 East. In 1.6 miles, turn right on Blackburn Road; in 0.4 mile, turn left into the parking lot across from Rippon Lodge. GPS: N38 36.686' / W77 16.815'

## The Hike

Captain John Smith explored Neabsco Creek in 1608. The name is derived from a Doeg Indian village that was here, Niopsco. As more settlers came into this region, the area became a commercial waterway throughout most of the eighteenth century. As the area grew, soil runoff from nearby farms and the loss of trees due to nearby farms and industry turned Neabsco Creek from a passable waterway into a wetland. Today the Julie Metz Wetland Preserve is a thriving habitat for beavers, snakes, turtles, and many varieties of waterfowl, including ducks, sparrows, and great blue herons.

The newest link in the Potomac Heritage National Scenic Trail is the Neabsco Creek Boardwalk in Woodbridge. Built over the creek, it is designed to provide viewing access to the creek's animals and plants without disturbing them. Each end of the boardwalk has a large deck space big enough for everyone to observe the wildlife and vegetation up close—even whole classes. Neabsco Creek is a tidal marsh of the Potomac River, so the scenery changes slightly depending on the time of day and the season. This hike is almost entirely without shade, so be aware of that if you head out in the middle of the day, especially during summer.

The boardwalk, which opened in June 2019, links important historic sites as well. Across from the parking area is Rippon Lodge, which dates to 1747 and is one of the oldest houses in Prince William County. Also near here is the site of the Neabsco Iron Works, the first iron manufacturer in Northern Virginia. It opened in the 1730s and closed almost one hundred years later. The operation of the ironworks required copious amounts of timber, and these were taken from the area that is now the wetland.

Just 20 minutes north of Neabsco Creek is the picturesque town of Occoquan. Located on the banks of the Occoquan River, it began as a mill town in the 1700s and is today a thriving artist community with many shops and restaurants. An annual fall art festival is held, usually in late September.

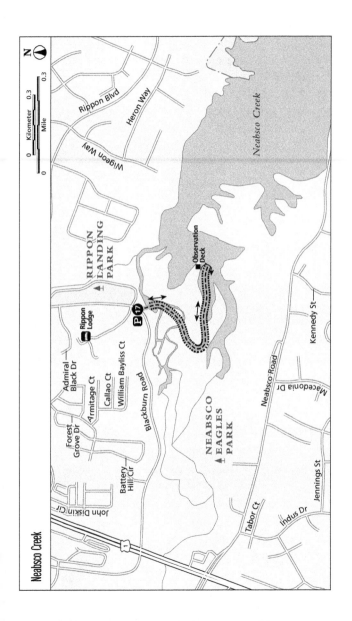

Neabsco Creek

# Miles and Directions

**0.0** Begin at the parking lot and take the paved path to the boardwalk.

**0.1** Walk onto the boardwalk.

**0.7** Arrive at the large deck at the end of the boardwalk. Turn around and return the same way.

**1.5** Arrive back at the parking lot.

# 18  Lake Accotink

This park provides a peaceful getaway into the woods and by the water, but it is very convenient to residential areas, making it perfect for a quick respite after work or on the weekend.

**Main interest:** Nature, bird watching
**Distance:** 3.9-mile loop
**Hiking time:** About 2 hours
**Difficulty:** Easy
**Trail surface:** Paved and natural surfaces
**Best season:** Year-round
**Other trail users:** Runners, cyclists
**Canine compatibility:** Dogs allowed on leash
**Fees and permits:** None

**Schedule:** Daily dawn to dusk
**Facilities:** Restrooms, drinking water, picnic tables, playground
**Map:** www.fairfaxcounty.gov/ parks/sites/parks/files/assets/ documents/waterfront/lake accotink/lake-accotink-loop-trail -map.pdf
**Trail contact:** Lake Accotink Park, 7500 Accotink Park Rd., Spring-field 22150; (703) 569-3464; www.fairfaxcounty.gov/parks/ lake-accotink/trails

**Finding the Trailhead:** From I-495 South, take exit 54A-B onto Braddock Road. Keep left and turn onto Braddock Road. In 2 miles, turn right onto Backlick Road and then in 1.5 miles turn right on Highland Street. Bear right onto Accotink Park Road and straight to the parking lot. GPS: N38 7942' / W77 2192'

## The Hike

In the middle of a busy suburb, Lake Accotink and its surrounding park is a quiet place to wind down after a workday or spend an early weekend morning. The land that now includes Lake Accotink Park was given to William Fitzhugh in the late 1600s. Accotink refers to the largest Native American village originally located here, but Fitzhugh called the area Ravensworth and built a plantation home. The Fitzhugh and the Lee families were related, and the Lees often visited here. In fact, Robert E. Lee and his wife, Mary Custis Lee, granddaughter of George Washington, spent part of their honeymoon at Ravensworth. The land was sold off in smaller parcels after the war, and one of those sections became Lake Accotink Park. The lake was created in 1918 by a dam on Accotink Creek and was designed to provide water for the US Army at Fort Belvoir. By the 1950s, the water became too polluted because of a nearby sewage plant, and the reservoir was closed. Fairfax County purchased the lake and surrounding land in 1964, a total of 224 acres, to develop for recreation. Unfortunately, the pollution issues continued, and the lake had to be closed in 1970. The sewage plant also closed. In 1971, the county decided to drain and refill the lake and stock it with fish. The park now offers canoe and rowboat rentals, but swimming is not recommended. In the near future, the county plans to dredge the lake to an even 8-foot depth. The trail skirts the lake and goes out into the park area, except for a small portion that goes onto the road by a school.

From the parking lot, join the trail. Soon you will walk under a trestle bridge of the Norfolk Southern Railway, and you might hear a train passing overhead. Along the way, look for markers highlighting the history of this area, for example, portions of the trail were originally part of the Orange and Alexandria Railway used during the Civil War. At the beginning of the trail, a steep hill leads you into the woods. At Lonsdale Drive, walk about 3 blocks past the elementary school, and rejoin the trail. From there a set of stairs leads

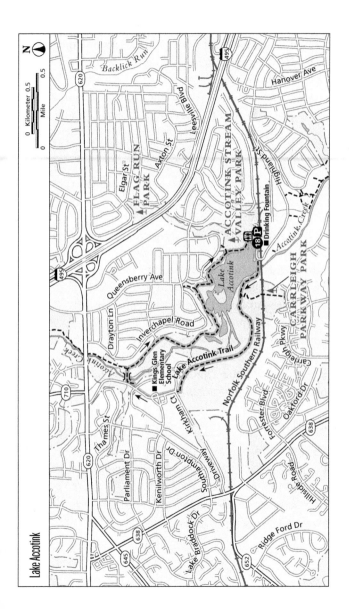

Lake Accotink

down to a bridge that crosses Accotink Creek, and the trail turns right along the other side of the lake. Around the water, look for Canada geese, osprey, skinks, and turtles. Bald eagles have been seen as well.

Lake Accotink Trail is part of the Gerry Connolly Cross County Trail, a 40-mile multiuse trail that goes across Fairfax County. It's about 30 minutes from Old Town Alexandria and 30 minutes from Old Town Fairfax. Both are nice places to relax with a meal or just some ice cream after your hike. See www.visitalexandriava.com/ and www.fairfaxva.gov/ for more information about both. Also about a 30-minute drive away are Woodlawn Plantation and the Pope-Leighey House. Woodlawn was part of Mount Vernon until Washington gave the land to his nephew Lawrence Lewis, who married Nelly Custis, granddaughter of Martha Washington. In 1846, it was sold to Quakers who operated the plantation with only freed workers, making a political statement in slaveholding Virginia. On the grounds is the Frank Lloyd Wright's Pope-Leighey House, which was moved here from Falls Church, Virginia, to keep it from being bulldozed during the construction of I-66. More information can be found at www .woodlawnpopeleighey.org/.

## Miles and Directions

- **0.0** Join the trailhead at the parking lot.
- **1.3** Cross Rolling Road and walk 3 blocks on the sidewalk to the continuation of the trail.
- **1.6** Cross Accotink Creek and turn right to follow the trail.
- **3.9** Arrive back at the parking lot.

# 19 Lake Anne

Celebrate one man's vision of the perfect place to live at this small lake with a planned community surrounding it.

---

**Main interest:** Nature, water views

**Distance:** 1.5-mile loop

**Hiking time:** About 1 hour

**Difficulty:** Easy

**Trail surface:** Natural surfaces

**Best season:** Year-round

**Other trail users:** Runners

**Canine compatibility:** Dogs allowed on leash

**Fees and permits:** None

**Schedule:** Daily dawn to dusk

**Facilities:** None, but restrooms available at the museum and at restaurants if you are a customer.

**Map:** www.restonpaths.com/Lake Anne/Images/LakeAnneMap.pdf

**Trail contact:** Reston Association, 12001 Sunrise Valley Dr., Reston 20191; (703) 435-6530; reston.org

---

**Finding the Trailhead:** From the Dulles Toll Road, VA 267, take exit 13 onto Wiehle Road (VA 828). Turn right on Wiehle Road and in 1.6 miles, turn left on North Shore Drive. In 0.3 mile, turn left at the sign for Lake Anne and go to the large parking lot. GPS: N38 9699' / W77 3409'

## The Hike

The town of Reston was designed in 1964 by Robert E. Simon, who envisioned a developed community where there were schools, recreation areas, shopping, and businesses and everyone would have equal access to all amenities. His motto was "Work, Play, Live," and the idea was that the town would have everything one would need for a happy life. He based his idea on seven principles, which included a variety of housing for all income levels and ages, a focus on cultural and recreational activities available to all, and beautiful design in nature and in building. Part of this vision is the 55 miles of walking trails throughout Reston and the four man-made lakes, such as Lake Anne.

The lake is fed by Difficult Run and is a popular spot all year, but particularly in summer, when the adjacent plaza has lots of outdoor events. The Saturday farmers' market, evening concerts, and outdoor dining are all great reasons to visit Lake Anne. The walk around the lake is a fun way to stretch your legs after a meal or to work up an appetite.

The trail begins at the village plaza past Huron House and turns right to follow the water. Cross over a bridge, then stay right and walk up to Waterview Cluster and turn left on the sidewalk to rejoin the trail. Continue to follow the trail, always bearing left to follow the lake. The trail varies from asphalt to sidewalk throughout the walk. As you make the left-hand turn at Inlet Court, you might see people launching off to paddleboard. Lake Anne is a great place for this activity, especially for beginner paddleboarders because the water is very calm. The trail ends back at Lake Anne Village, where you can spend some time relaxing with a coffee or something to eat.

Near the village is the Reston Historic Trust and Museum, which is worth a stop. Check their hours and other information at www.restonmuseum.org/.

## Miles and Directions

**0.0**   Begin at the west end of Lake Anne Village Plaza and pass Huron House.

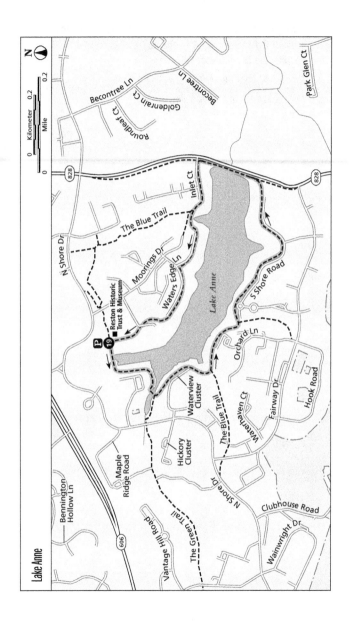

Lake Anne

**0.1** Turn right to join the trail. Cross the bridge and continue through Waterview Cluster as the trail goes around the lake, keeping the lake on your left.

**1.1** Turn left at Inlet Court.

**1.5** Arrive back at Lake Anne Village.

# 20 Bears Den Overlook

This hike features a portion of the Appalachian Trail known as the "roller coaster" for its miles of ups and downs. This section, however, is fairly even, making it a great trail for anyone.

**Main interest:** History, nature, scenic views

**Distance:** 1.4-mile loop

**Hiking time:** About 1.5 hours

**Difficulty:** Easy

**Trail surface:** Natural surfaces, a short amount of rough trail over rocks

**Best season:** Year-round; if the weather is very cold, the trail can be icy.

**Other trail users:** None

**Canine compatibility:** Dogs allowed on leash

**Fees and permits:** $3 for parking

**Schedule:** Daily 8 a.m. to 9 p.m.

**Facilities:** Restrooms, picnic area

**Map:** www.hikingupward.com/OVH/BearsDenOverlook/

**Trail contact:** Bears Den, 18393 Blue Ridge Mountain Rd., Bluemont 20135; (540) 554-8708; www.bearsdencenter.org/

**Finding the Trailhead:** From VA 7 West, continue driving, bypassing Leesburg. After about 17 miles, turn left onto Blue Ridge Mountain Road. Follow this for 0.5 mile to the parking lot. GPS: N39 06.613' / W77 51.246'

## The Hike

The highlight of this trail is an overlook where you can see across the DC Metro area to the Blue Ridge Mountains in West Virginia. Historians believe the overlook could have been used by Native Americans as a directional navigation spot. Another theory is that it was used to mark the changes of season on early Indian calendars.

The overlook is near historic Bears Den Lodge. Built in the 1930s by a prominent D.C. doctor, Huron Lawson, and his wife, Francesca Kaspari, an opera singer, the lodge was designed to look like a medieval castle. A rounded wall on one side was created for its acoustics and became Francesca's music studio. The couple used the lodge as a summer home and charged visitors a nickel to visit their petting zoo and to access the overlook. After the couple passed away in the 1960s, the property changed hands a few times before it was purchased by the Appalachian Trail Conservancy, and the castle was opened as a hiker hostel. Today the property is still used by hikers and can also be rented by other groups for retreats, parties, or other uses. The castle can be seen at the end of this hike, and the surrounding grounds are a peaceful place to hang out before heading back.

To start the hike, join the Nature Trail at the west side of the parking lot. Walk through a picnic and camping area before heading down some rustic stairs and bearing right and back uphill. Follow the trail to the Blue Blaze Loop and bear left through the trees until you see the opening on your left that leads to the overlook. The short walk down is rocky but easy to manage. Spend some time enjoying this incredible view. The overlook area has two sections of rocks and plenty of places to sit and take in the scenery. The Shenandoah Valley stretches out to the Blue Ridge Mountains in the distance. Off to the left you can see the outer suburbs of Washington, D.C. In fall and spring the colors throughout the valley are amazing. While this spot is spectacular anytime, it's very popular at sunset. If you do come then, you'll want to bring a headlamp or flashlight and head straight back to the parking lot afterward.

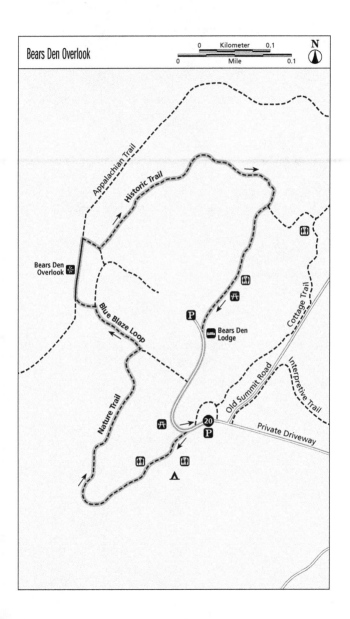

There are several wineries in the area near Bears Den, and many are listed on the Loudoun County Snickers Gap Cluster (www.visitloudoun.org/drink/wine-country/clusters/). Also, just after the turnoff from Route 7 to get to this hike is a great brewery. Historic Leesburg is a 30-minute drive from here as well. Visit www.leesburgva.gov/ for more information.

## Miles and Directions

**0.0** Begin at the Nature Trail, located on the west side of the parking lot. Follow this through the campground and as it bears right.

**0.3** Turn left on the Blue Blaze Loop until you see the sign for the overlook, then turn left.

**0.7** From the overlook, turn left on the Appalachian Trail until you see the sign for the Historic Trail.

**0.8** Turn right and follow the Historic Trail to the Bears Den Lodge.

**1.3** Arrive at the lodge grounds. Walk past the lodge down the gravel road back to the parking lot.

**1.4** Arrive back at the parking lot

# 21 Leesylvania State Park

This hike wanders through what was once an estate owned by the Lee family of Virginia. Many of the family members played pivotal roles in our nation's history.

**Main interest:** History, nature
**Distance:** 2-mile loop
**Hiking time:** About 2 hours
**Difficulty:** Easy to moderate
**Trail surface:** Natural surfaces
**Best season:** Year-round
**Other trail users:** None
**Canine compatibility:** Dogs allowed on leash
**Fees and permits:** $7 per car
**Schedule:** Mon to Fri 6 a.m. to 30 minutes past sunset; Sat and Sun 5 a.m. to 30 minutes past sunset
**Facilities:** Restrooms
**Map:** www.dcr.virginia.gov/state-parks/document/data/trail-guide-leesylvania.pdf
**Trail contact:** Leesylvania State Park, 2001 Daniel K. Ludwig Dr., Woodbridge 22191; (703) 730-8205; www.dcr.virginia.gov/state-parks/leesylvania

**Finding the Trailhead:** From I-495 South, take the exit to I-95 South toward Richmond. In 13 miles, take exit 156 toward Rippon Landing. In 0.5 mile, keep left toward Dale Blvd. In about 2 miles, turn right on US 1/Richmond Highway, then in 1 mile, turn left onto Neabsco Road. In 2 miles, turn right into the park. Follow the road to the last parking lot. GPS: N38 58.934' / W77 26.350'

## The Hike

In the mid–1700s, Henry Lee II and his wife settled on this beautiful parcel of land right along the Potomac River. Here they raised eight children, one of whom was Henry "Lighthorse" Lee, a governor of Virginia, a congressman, and

Revolutionary War hero. He was also the father of Robert E. Lee, the commander of the Confederate forces during the American Civil War. In 1825, the land was sold to Henry Fairfax, a member of a prominent local family. During the Civil War, the land was used for Confederate encampments due to its proximity to Washington, D.C., across the river. Artilleries were set up on bluffs by the river, including at Freestone Point, where the hike begins. After the war, the property was rented out to various groups until 1978, when the property was purchased and donated to the Virginia State Parks.

After the First Battle of Bull Run, Confederate forces established artillery points along the Potomac River to keep the Union army from bringing supplies up the river to Washington, D.C. Three cannons were set up at Freestone Point between Quantico and Neabsco Creeks. There was only one battle fought from this point. Recent studies have determined that five slaves escaped from Leesylvania in September 1861 to the Union ship USS *Seminole* and informed them of the Confederates holding at Freestone Point. They attacked but the battle was short and ended with no clear victor. The Union, however, was now aware of the Confederate strategy along the river. The park commemorates this battle every September. Other events and programs are offered throughout the year, including guided walks, nature classes, and boat tours.

Begin your hike by walking down to Freestone Point to see the cannons. From there, walk inland and follow the red blazes for the Lee's Woods Trail. You will pass a two-story brick chimney, which is the only remaining part of the Lee-Fairfax home. There is also a small cemetery with family graves. The trail also provides beautiful views of the Potomac River.

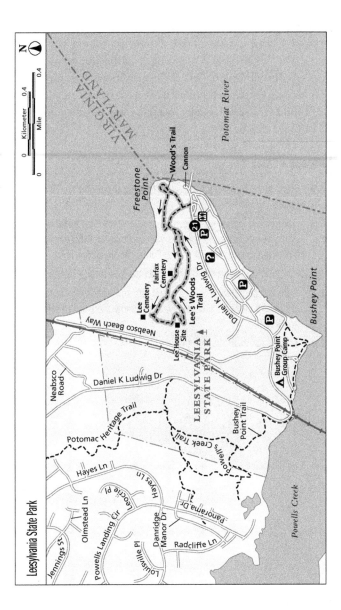

Leesylvania State Park

N

Potomac River

MARYLAND
VIRGINIA

Freestone Point

Wood's Trail

Cannon

Fairfax Cemetery

Lee Cemetery

Neabsco Beach Way

Lee House Site

Lee's Woods Trail

Daniel K Ludwig Dr

21

P

?

P

P

Bushey Point

Bushey Point Group Camp

LEESYLVANIA STATE PARK

Neabsco Road

Daniel K Ludwig Dr

Potomac Heritage Trail

Hayes Ln

Leoctrie Pl

Hayes Ln

Danridge Manor Dr

Panorama Dr

Radcliffe Ln

Jennings St

Olmstead Ln

Powell's Landing Cir

Louisville Pl

Bushey Point Trail

Powell's Creek Trail

Powells Creek

0    Kilometer    0.4
0    Mile    0.4

Leesylvania is a 30-minute drive from Gunston Hall, the home of George Mason, a key figure in shaping the new nation. The house and gardens are available for tours, and there is continuing archeological excavation. The grounds overlook the Potomac River at Mason Neck State Park and are a wonderful spot to enjoy a picnic lunch. Visit gunston hall.org/ for details.

## Miles and Directions

**0.0** Start at the parking lot and walk to the cannons at Freestone Point.

**0.5** From Freestone Point, walk past the amphitheater to the Lee's Woods trailhead marked with red blazes. Take the right fork and continue up hill to the Fairfax family cemetery.

**1.0** Continue up to the top of the hill to the Lee family cemetery.

**1.2** From the cemetery, the trail bears left and heads back. Stop at the two-story brick chimney. Then follow the path to the trail's end.

**2.0** Arrive back at the parking area.

# 22 Red Rock Wilderness

A blend of history and nature greet you on this trail as you walk past the ruins of nineteenth-century farm buildings to a scenic spot overlooking the Potomac River.

**Main interest:** Nature, history
**Distance:** 1.2-mile loop
**Hiking time:** About 2 hours
**Difficulty:** Easy
**Trail surface:** Natural surfaces
**Best season:** Year-round
**Other trail users:** Runners
**Canine compatibility:** Dogs allowed on leash
**Fees and permits:** None
**Schedule:** Daily dawn to dusk

**Facilities:** None
**Map:** www.novaparks.com/sites/default/files/maps/RedckMap.pdf
**Trail contact:** Red Rock Wilderness Overlook Regional Park, 43098 Edwards Ferry Rd., Leesburg 20176; (703) 779-9372; www.novaparks.com/parks/red-rock-wilderness-overlook-regional-park

**Finding the Trailhead:** From VA 7 West, turn right on River Creek Parkway, about 5 miles after the intersection with VA 28. In 2 miles, the road bears left and becomes Edwards Ferry Road. The parking lot will be on your right. GPS: N39 1127' / W77 5100'

## The Hike

In addition to spectacular views of the Potomac River, this park has several ruins of buildings belonging to the estate of Charles Paxton, a wealthy man from Leesburg. Among the remains are a granary, a well house, and an ice house where blocks of ice from the frozen river were stored. The Paxtons lived on a large property called Carlheim in Leesburg, which was adjacent to the park. The land and buildings were

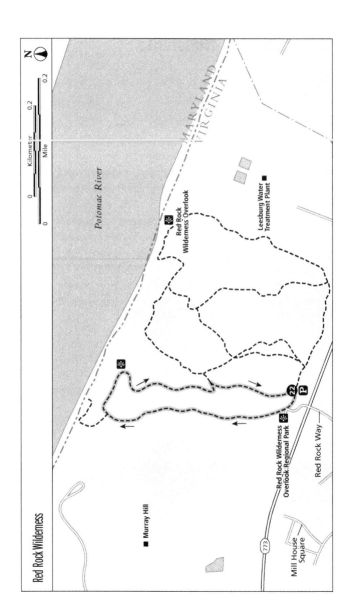

Red Rock Wilderness

Potomac River

Red Rock Wilderness Overlook

Leesburg Water Treatment Plant

MARYLAND
VIRGINIA

Murray Hill

Red Rock Wilderness Overlook Regional Park

22
P

Red Rock Way

Mill House Square

773

N

Kilometer

Mile

0    0.2

0    0.2

used for a creamery run by the Paxtons. Historical markers describe each of the ruins throughout the park. The land was acquired by NOVA Regional Park Authority in 1978. Carlheim House is now an organization for people with disabilities, per the request of Mrs. Paxton.

From the parking lot, take a look at the granary and stable buildings and then proceed on the hike. Look for the white blazes and follow the path. The dirt trail crosses over a stream via a bridge before becoming steep as you head down to the river. Be careful and take your time. The trail turns right along a bluff over the river for a bit until it heads up to the overlook. Take some time to enjoy the view that, on a clear day, stretches across the river to the C&O Canal on the Maryland side. From there, continue on the white trail until it intersects with the green trail, which will lead you back to the parking lot. Take a look at the old ice house on the way.

Red Rock Wilderness is very close to the town of Leesburg. Established more than 250 years ago, Leesburg is now a charming city with historic sites and wonderful shops and restaurants. Visit www.leesburgva.gov/ for more information. Several wineries and breweries are nearby as well.

## Miles and Directions

**0.0**    Begin the trail by the granary building and follow the white marks.

**0.5**    At the river, turn right to the overlook.

**0.6**    From the overlook, head back inland, following the trail.

**0.9**    Turn onto the green trail toward the ice house.

**1.2**    Arrive back at the parking lot.

# About the Author

Louise Baxter is a freelance writer living in the Washington, D.C., area. She is the author of *Best Easy Day Hikes Washington, D.C.* and has written for the *Washington Post, Travel Weekly,* Yahoo Travel, and other publications. She writes primarily about the mid-Atlantic region covering travel-related subjects. She spent 11 years working in the tour and travel field, planning and operating tours throughout North America. Louise is also an ESL (English as a Second Language) teacher and an editor.